For chef and tastemaker Woldy Reyes, cooking is a celebration of identity. Growing up in Southern California as a first-generation Filipino American, Woldy felt like an outsider, always straddling two worlds. At home, his family ate adobo with rice, gathered in the kitchen to roll lumpia, and roasted a whole goat in the backyard to make kalderetang kambing (celebratory goat stew). At school, all he wanted were Lunchables and Flamin' Hot Cheetos.

It wasn't until he discovered the power of food as a means of connection—to strangers and friends, to his heritage, and even to himself—that he began cooking in earnest and sharing his story through the dishes he made. His signature style, now beloved by his catering clients in New York City and beyond, highlights classic Filipino food but renders it lighter, fresher, and plant driven, with an emphasis on feeling nourished and wholesome.

In the Kusina is Woldy's story as told through a collection of vibrant, vegetable-forward Filipino recipes. These aren't your lola's traditional dishes; here, Filipino tastes and techniques are reimagined for a new generation of home cooks, resulting in a trove of elegant and boldly flavorful recipes organized by season:

- Asparagus Lumpia with Herby Fish Sauce makes the perfect springtime snack.

- Revel in the bounty of summer produce with Sungold and Pipino salad.

- Celebrate fall with a cozy Bibingka Apple Bread with Maple Glaze.

- Pair warming Sotanghon Soup with a fresh Radish and Herb Salad with Sweet Buttered Nuts for a healthful winter meal.

- Plus, a chapter of foundational sauces and pantry items—Coconut Hot Sauce, Peanut Salsa, Seedy Chili Oil—elevates any dish.

Brimming with gorgeous photos of food that's as lovely to look at as it is to eat, this is more than just a carefully curated selection of dishes. *In the Kusina* is a joyful story told in Woldy's charming voice, a love letter to Filipino food and flavors, and, most of all, a cooking reference filled with delicious recipes that you'll turn to again and again.

KUSI

in the

NA

My Seasonal Filipino Cooking

Woldy Reyes

PHOTOGRAPHY BY **FUJIO EMURA**

CHRONICLE BOOKS
SAN FRANCISCO

Library of Congress Cataloging-in-Publication Data available.

ISBN 978-1-7972-2784-9

Manufactured in China.

Creative direction by Woldy Reyes.
Photography by Fujio Emura.
Creative production by Tara Thomas.
Food styling by LJ Almendras and Tony Ortiz.
Prop styling by Sasha Verovka.
Photo assistance by Seth Kenji.
Prop assistance by Lauryn Holmquist and Kate Atkinson.
Ghostwriting by Max Berlinger.
Design by Lizzie Vaughan.
Illustrations on page 19 and 270 by Arsh Raziuddin.

10 9 8 7 6 5 4 3 2 1

Chronicle books and gifts are available at special quantity
discounts to corporations, professional associations, literacy
programs, and other organizations. For details and discount
information, please contact our premiums department at
corporatesales@chroniclebooks.com or at 1-800-759-0190.

Chronicle Books LLC
680 Second Street
San Francisco, California 94107
www.chroniclebooks.com

Contents

Introduction

42 Sawsawan

Sauces, Condiments, Pickles, and Pantry Items

70 Winter

Family, Nostalgia, and a Warm Bowl of Rice Porridge

124   Spring

A Time of Renewal, a Time to Watch Things Grow

166 Summer

Summer Is a Party, Summer Is Casual, Summer Is Abundance

222 Fall

Caterer to Chef to Community

GROWING UP:

The Filipino American Experience

Defining identity is so complex. My identity comprises so many different things—I'm a first-generation Filipino American, I'm gay, I have a disability, and, growing up, I was overweight. One of the strongest memories I have from my childhood was feeling that I didn't have a voice. I have a twin brother who is deaf, and I'm hard of hearing. When we were in school, he was put in a class for the deaf children, while I was left alone in a classroom with hearing kids. But I had to wear a device that looked like headphones with a harness strapped to my chest that announced I had a disability. Rather than speak for myself, I used sign language and the interpreter they assigned me as a means to shield myself from my own voice. My fear was that speaking would reveal the truth of who I was— that I was queer, that I was deaf. I was scared it would show my otherness, the ways that I was different. As a child, I spent a lot of time trying to make myself as invisible and small as possible.

The one place I liked to be while at school was in the cafeteria. I remember things like canned green beans and carrots being dumped into the food and thinking, *This is so cool*. Food represented all the different parts of my identity, though in some ways, it also highlighted these differences. At home, I would eat Filipino food with my immigrant family, but then at school I'd see Hot Pockets, Doritos, and Flamin' Hot Cheetos (my favorite). I always wanted my parents to send me to school with lunch money instead of food from home—I didn't want the kids at school to see what my mom made for me, dishes like steamed rice with a pungent-smelling adobo. I wanted to just eat, like, a hamburger. I wanted to hide who I was at home and just be an "American" kid with Lunchables, Goldfish crackers, and peanut butter and jelly sandwiches in my lunch bag.

It was in high school that I started to watch cooking shows on the Food Network with gusto. Rachael Ray, Martha Stewart, Nigella Lawson, Ina Garten: all those women left such a strong impression on me. I was mesmerized by the way they moved, the way they talked as they cooked; it was a total escape. They were so aspirational, and their shows got me excited about the idea of entertaining.

I nurtured this interest by cooking for my family. One of the first things I made was a tiered birthday cake for my lola, my grandmother. It was from a boxed cake mix, and I frosted it and put flowers on it. Looking back, I think it probably looked like a wedding cake. I was fixated on making it perfect for her. When I brought it out, everyone was taking pictures of it and oohing and aahing—the satisfaction was addictive. Another time, I made my aunt and uncle dinner for their wedding anniversary. I chose the menu, picked the platters, and created a tablescape. Catering to people and serving them food was exciting to me.

When I moved to New York in 2010, right after college, I worked in the fashion industry for a few years—at PR firms, at publications like *Elle* and *Nylon*, and for the designer Phillip Lim in a variety of roles. I've always had a love of fashion and style. Beauty and self-expression are really important to me. Sometimes fashion can be seen as superficial, but I think that wanting to add beauty to the world is a really noble aspiration.

The fashion world was quite taxing, though, so I started to pivot to food, first by working catering jobs, which gave me a glimpse at not only the behind-the-scenes creative process of inventing fab dishes, but also the logistical elements, which are fascinating and crucial to running a successful business. From there I started catering small parties and events for the friends I had made in the fashion industry. Over time, the cadence and size of the events I was catering increased, and eventually, I opened my business, Woldy Kusina.

I've been blessed that this path, though a little twisty, ultimately brought together two of my great loves: fashion and food. There's actually a lot of overlap between them in the way I cook and present food, with an emphasis on a lovely, graceful presentation. My dishes are filtered through the lens of my queerness, and I like to impart on them a sense of whimsy, something alluring, and a heavy dose of feminine energy. So, that's how my journey led me here, to this cookbook.

Writing this book was like a full-on therapy session. As I was combing through all the meals I had as a kid, all the celebrations, all the events I attended and catered, memories came flooding back to me. I was laughing. I was crying. I was feeling all the things! But two moments really shaped the way I think about food and prepare it today, even though they could not be more different.

The first is when my father brought my twin brother and me on a trip to a local farm where we helped him pick out a live goat (!!) that was butchered on-site and handed back to us in a neatly wrapped package. How wild is that? I mean, I grew up in the suburbs of Los Angeles, not a rural area. Despite the experience being a little off-putting, it was the essence of farm-to-table cooking before it was trendy. Before you call PETA on me, please know that there is no meat in this book! And, honestly, when it does come to eating meat, it doesn't get more sustainable than that.

We did this for every family celebration, holiday, and birthday, and after our chosen goat was butchered, we would come home and my dad would simmer the meat for hours in a big pot out in the backyard with sautéed onions and a lot of garlic. I remember this baffling, robust smell perfuming the air. My family was just so unapologetically Filipino; they didn't care what the neighbors thought! I smile to think about those nights because they capture the spirit of Filipino cooking perfectly.

My favorite part was when we all sat together and feasted on the decadent meal, the Filipino specialty called kalderetang kambing (celebratory goat stew). It's this deep, rich terra cotta–colored stew filled with warming spices served over rice. I found that meal so comforting as a kid.

The other moment that looms large in my mind is a total 180. It's the time I spent in my lola's verdant, leafy, magical garden. She was so proud of that space. I was absolutely amazed at the way she'd be cooking something in the kitchen and then she'd go out to the garden, snip-snip something, and come back in and use it right then. Watching food go, literally, from ground to stove to plate left a powerful impression on me. I feel echoes of it today when I visit roadside farm stands near my house in upstate New York (or take a stab at gardening myself—it's a slow and ongoing process). It's these two recollections that have fueled so much of my career as a chef and led me to write this book.

As I started to work on the book, I realized that these recipes originate from those two memories—the traditional meals I grew up with, but with a more vegetable-forward approach and an emphasis on fresh, seasonal ingredients. The end result is that you'll learn not only about classic Filipino cuisine but also a bit of my own personal tastes. Cooking is, after all, a form of biography, and I hope that with each dish, a little bit of my history shines through.

Being part of people's important milestones feels good. Through food, I can connect with people, be part of their lives, and bring them joy. Today, I've found my voice through cooking and food, and I use it as a way to highlight all the different parts of myself, not hide them. You can see it in the flavors that I like to use; they're bold: sweet, sour, salty, and spicy. I use bright, flamboyant colors. I'm no longer trying to straddle two worlds—I'm in my own lane. I'm not trying to do what everybody else is doing. It's been a long journey to get here, but now I embrace being loud and proud, and I want my cooking to reflect that. I'm no longer ashamed of who I am, and my food represents that.

Vegetable-Forward, Seasonal *Cooking*

First and foremost, *In the Kusina* is all about bringing Filipino flavors into every kitchen. I conceived this book for everyone: Filipino cooks, non-Filipino cooks, and Filipinos who don't usually cook Filipino food. But it's not a straightforward look at our cuisine. It takes traditional dishes and updates them for a modern palate, rendering them lighter, fresher, seasonal, and more plant-driven, with an emphasis on feeling nourished and wholesome.

I was inspired, in part, by the fact that people have grown more mindful about eating less meat, and by the shift toward plant-based menus at restaurants around me. A few years ago, I bought a house in upstate New York, and seeing all the incredible farms there also opened my eyes to the way I ate and made me think about how I might impart some of the things I learned into my own recipes. I began wondering what would happen if I swapped the ratios, so the vegetables and produce were the stars of the show and animal proteins were just sides or garnishes.

This added to the fact that, when I first started cooking professionally, it was often for people in the fashion world. I tried to craft meals that were light, beautiful, and pleasing to the eye. The reaction was amazing. As I became more confident, I wanted to integrate more of myself into the food I was preparing. How would I eat it? How would I enjoy it?

Finding ways to eat more whole foods and cook more meals centered around produce has become an obsession of mine. Although I do still eat meat, and proudly so, I have shifted the way I think of meat—more as a special occasion ingredient, not a go-to or a necessity. In this book, I've left out meat altogether, focusing on salads, soups, mains, and desserts that let produce shine and still sing with flavor.

Vegetable-forward cooking asks you to pay attention to the seasons. I recently listened to Alice Waters on a podcast, and she was talking about her approach, or philosophy, really, to eating and cooking, which she famously learned during her first visit to France. Boiled down, it's eating with the seasons: Nature tells you what to eat if you listen closely enough. She believes that cooking seasonally not only makes for more flavorful food, but also reverses health issues and helps address the climate crisis. Listening to her talk, I was taken with how simple she made it sound. It's so obvious! The earth has seasons and cycles, and it gives you what you need at any given moment. It's what ancient Indigenous cultures have always known and done. It was both so self-evident and yet so wise.

I realized that I had been developing a version of that same philosophy myself over the years. Growing up in California, you're a bit spoiled; the seasons aren't as extreme, and you get a pretty diverse bounty of freshly grown produce year-round—a tomato in January isn't really a big deal. But when I moved to New York, and later, when I began to frequent farmers' markets, I started to see the way the seasons bring you different fare at different times, and the elegance of that. There is something undeniably beautiful about the fact that a tomato has a distinctly rich, sweet flavor at the end of the summer. Sure, nowadays you can buy a tomato any time of the year, but you're always chasing that ineffable fresh, bright taste it gives when it's at its peak.

There's a romance to always pursuing that seasonal abundance, to making the most of what's currently available, knowing that it won't last. It's why people get so obsessed with gardening, recognizing that you can't control nature; instead, you must be patient and try to align yourself with it. It takes humility to know that we must work within nature's own rhythms but that, if we do, we get some amazing rewards. Think about the way a juicy peach tastes in the summer—the glamorous pink-orange flesh, the fuzzy skin, the juice as it drips down your chin, the mind-boggling flavor. That's nature showing off, telling you that your timing is perfect. Think about the heft and complexity of a sweet potato in fall, when your body craves that rootedness to prepare for the colder months. Or the tannic bite of a green onion in spring, signaling rebirth. This is nature talking to you, rewarding you for your patience.

This philosophy has deeply informed the way I approach eating and cooking today. I've taken dishes and flavors that I grew up with and adapted them to this fresh, seasonal style of cooking because, frankly, it seems like the only way that makes sense. And it's not just the way I cook, but the way I eat too—in a slower, more thoughtful manner, with the intention of nourishing my body, not just filling it up. I'm nowhere near perfect, but I do think that cooking and eating like this is my small way of making an impact, and hopefully this book will encourage you to think about how you approach food too. To attempt to live your life more closely to nature is an honorable, noble thing, and I hope that this book can help point you in that direction.

Introduction

My Seven *Guiding* Principles *to* Modern Filipino *Cooking*

I am all about taking the traditional Filipino flavors and dishes I grew up with and updating them, usually by adding in some things I've learned in my years as a caterer and personal cook in New York. From working alongside a dizzying array of incredibly talented cooks and chefs, I've learned about contemporary culinary techniques and global influences, which now show up in my own food. My dishes honor, and even celebrate, the rich culinary heritage of the Philippines while incorporating new and innovative flavors. With my cooking, I aim to captivate the senses, elevate the entire dining experience, and showcase the dynamic and evolving nature of Filipino cuisine. I've been working on this for years, fine-tuning my repertoire and testing it out on friends, family, and clients, at parties that I'm hired to cater and pop-ups I'm invited to take part in. And while working on this book, I saw that my cooking philosophy, as it were (which is really a fancy term for the loose set of rules I fall back on when I'm feeling lost or stuck), can be boiled down to seven guiding principles or elements.

My hope is that this book finds its way into the hands and homes of people who have little or no experience cooking Filipino food, as well as people who love Filipino food already but are looking for a lighter approach. And in using this book, I hope that you don't just follow the recipes, but gain a deeper understanding of the building blocks of modern Filipino cuisine and start playing around with them, applying certain flavors or techniques to your everyday repertoire. I want to help you become a more confident cook in your own kitchen, not someone who needs to follow each step of a recipe exactly (but if that makes you happy, be my guest). The thrill of making new dishes has been one of the joys of my life, and if I can pass that on, my heart will explode with joy!

So, without further ado, here they are. These are my guideposts for modern Filipino cooking (though I think they would also apply to most types of cooking). If you're ever stuck, come back to this section and remind yourself of the seven principles that will make any dish sing!

1 Bold and Vibrant

Bold and vibrant flavors awaken the palate. Modern Filipino cuisine is based on a combination of sweet, sour, salty, and spicy tastes, but with an eye on combining them to achieve a harmonious balance in each dish. No subtle, delicate flavors here! I want layers, contrasts, and zingy, fiery, audacious flavors that leave you saying, "Wow!"

2 Artfully Presented

Artistic elements and dramatic flourishes (that is very me!) elevate the dining experience. My dishes are thoughtfully plated, showcasing vibrant colors, unique textures, and creative arrangements. The presentation aims to be visually appealing, adding to the overall enjoyment of the meal. That doesn't mean fussy! A big stack of fried lumpia wrappers or a pile of roasted cabbage topped with a chunky, nutty gremolata can have the same amount of flair and excitement as something a bit more composed and regal!

3 Globally Influenced

Modern Filipino cuisine embraces global influences, incorporating ingredients and techniques from various culinary traditions. It may be infused with flavors from other Asian cuisines, such as Thai, Korean, or Japanese, or incorporate elements from Western cooking styles. I have been lucky enough to meet and cook alongside people of all races and nationalities, and they have, in turn, inspired me to consider techniques and flavors that I hadn't before. This is one of my favorite parts about living in a globalized, connected world, and specifically in New York. These culinary meetups have inspired some of the dishes you'll find in this book, and I think this fusion yields a unique and exciting twist on traditional Filipino dishes.

4 Light and Fresh

While still embracing the rich, savory, and powerful flavors of Filipino cuisine, modern Filipino food also emphasizes lightness and freshness. It incorporates a variety of fresh herbs, vegetables, and tropical flavors to add brightness and balance to the dishes. This emphasis on fresh ingredients adds a contemporary and wholesome aspect to the flavor profile, keeps in mind sustainability, and encourages cooks to choose things that are in season.

⁵ Full of Textural Contrast

Obviously, when you're cooking, flavor is top of mind, but modern Filipino food often includes a flirty, unexpected, and joyful play on textures. I really do believe these juxtapositions (think crunchy nuts on a creamy soup or roasted vegetables on a velvety, smooth sauce or juicy pickled raisins in a salad) elevate and enhance the dining experience—and frankly, they make it fun. By combining crispy, crunchy, and chewy elements in dishes, you create a delightful textural contrast that adds depth, novelty, interest, and excitement to your dining experience.

⁶ Sustainable and Locally Sourced

I think this goes for all cooking today, but my take on modern Filipino cuisine pays attention to sustainability and supports local producers whenever possible (I realize not everyone has access to small farms, but look online to see if there are any farmers' markets near you—you may be surprised!). It emphasizes the use of locally sourced and seasonal ingredients, promoting responsible, ethical, and eco-friendly dining. It also moves away from animal proteins and toward produce-centric meals. And while this element may seem separate from the flavor part of cooking, I can guarantee you it's not—you will see that local producers and in-season ingredients have earthier, richer, and deeper flavors.

⁷ With Unexpected Flair

Last but most definitely not least, modern Filipino cuisine is not afraid to push boundaries and experiment with unexpected flavors and combinations. It may incorporate unique ingredients, unconventional pairings, or innovative cooking techniques. This element of surprise and experimentation adds an exciting and contemporary twist to the food. One thing I've learned in the kitchen is that cooking should be fun—fun for the cook and for the diners. You want to create an atmosphere of joy and celebration around the entire experience. Everything involved in a meal—from the preparation to the cooking to the dining—should be filled with surprises, wonder, and happiness!

Stocking a Filipino American *Pantry*

The nice thing about Filipino food is you probably have a good deal of the go-to ingredients on hand, and with the addition of just a few extra pantry items, you'll be set up for success. There are a couple of things that may be a bit harder to find, but I think nowadays most major grocery stores have an "Asian foods" section, and there are Asian specialty markets in most bigger cities. And, yes, Amazon may be a big bad corporation, but it too often has some of the spices and hard-to-source items available if you can't find them anywhere else. I've also included my favorite brands in this list.

I hope that, with this book, you won't buy these extra ingredients just for the recipes here but will also start thinking about how they can work into your current repertoire. I hope you become more open to experimenting with Filipino flavors and curious to see what special concoctions you can dream up. You'll see that I am not strict in the kitchen—I have been influenced by so many things over the years, and I think playing around is the best part of being a cook. Be confident and brave and try new things! Cooking is like painting, and these ingredients are just some additional colors to add to your palette. Test them a few different ways and you'll end up with a beautiful picture.

Spices

Spices are the biggest difference between Eastern and Western cuisines, and they are essential to making Filipino cooking what it is. We rely on things like bay leaves, ginger, and peppercorns, which might be used more sparingly in other parts of the world. And yet they are such an easy way to expand the flavors you're already working with. Here are a few of the essential spices I use over and over in this book. (And OK, banana leaves are not technically a spice, but they add an aromatic note, not to mention an amazing presentation to any dish.) There's a certain sweet-spicy-sour flavor profile that grounds most Filipino cooking, and these are the keys to achieving that.

Banana leaves (Asian Best Frozen Banana Leaves)

Bay leaves

Black pepper

Coriander seeds

Ginger

Pink peppercorns

Red pepper (or chili) flakes

Vinegars

Vinegars are such an important part of Filipino cooking because they instantly add sharpness, tang, and brightness to a recipe. Their profile is a nice contrast to heavier dishes. Or just use them to add an extra layer of flavor. Cooking is all about balance and surprises. A healthy dose of acid elevates a lot of dishes, especially when used in sauces and marinades.

Apple cider vinegar

Cane vinegar (Datu Puti)

Rice vinegar (Marukan)

White vinegar

Oils

I'm sure you already have olive oil and butter in your kitchen, but I'd suggest adding these others to the mix, if they aren't already there. They're wonderful cooking fats, but also less neutral than other seed oils because they have a slight flavor to them, so by cooking with them, you're already setting the stage for a certain taste experience. Sesame oil is especially good for adding a nutty, earthy flavor to savory recipes like noodles and rice dishes. And while the same holds true for coconut oil, it's also great for sweet dishes and baking.

Avocado oil (Westbourne)

Neutral oil, such as canola or grapeseed

Sesame oil (Kadoya)

Unrefined coconut oil (Dr. Bronner's)

Coconut

Coconut is a huge part of the Filipino flavor palate—after all, it is a tropical country. And there are a bunch of ways to impart that flavor into a dish. Here are just a few of the ingredients that ensure the coconut vibes are strong, and I think once you start playing with these, you'll start adding them to more of your traditional Western recipes.

Coconut flakes (untoasted and unsweetened)

Coconut milk (Aroy-D)

Coconut palm sugar

Coconut yogurt (Cocojune)

Macapuno (Kamayan)

Soy Sauce versus Tamari

Soy sauce and tamari are very similar in a lot of ways, and some people use them interchangeably. They are both incredibly salty and add a lot of rich flavor to a sauce or marinade. Tamari is fermented longer, so it has a richer, deeper flavor. And, crucially, it's oftentimes (though not always) gluten-free, so it's a good option when cooking for people with those types of sensitivities.

Mushroom soy sauce (Healthy Boy)

Soy sauce (Datu Puti)

Sweet soy sauce (ABC Sweet Soy Sauce)

Tamari (San-J)

Flavor Bombs!

Perhaps my favorite section! These are exactly what they sound like—items that pack a lot of punch, whether it's spice, umami, salt, fishiness, or some mixture of them. Filipinos like a lot of bold, brassy flavors, and these ingredients easily and quickly make sure those flavors are present and accounted for. These flavor bombs can be part of another recipe (like sauces or marinades or dressings) or just dolloped on top of a dish as a shortcut to high-octane dining. Either way, expect lots and lots of audaciously delicious yumminess!

Banana ketchup (Jufran of UFC)

Chili Paste (page 45)

Patis, a.k.a. fish sauce (Rufina or Three Crabs)

Red miso (Hikari)

Sweet chili sauce (Mae Ploy)

Tahini (Seed and Mill)

Tamarind

White miso, preferably reduced sodium (Marukome)

Grains and Flours

I don't need to tell you that a great deal of Asian dishes are built around rice or noodles (as are many European dishes, but usually with different flavor profiles). Grains are sort of the backbone of Filipino cuisines—most dishes come with a side of rice or are served with noodles. They give meals a nourishing, grounding energy. I think some people think of grains as sides or superfluous, but they are not—they are deeply important parts of the eating experience, the balance to the vegetables or protein! Just like we need flavor contrast, we also need a contrast in terms of carbs versus fats versus protein. Incorporating grains ensures that when you're finished, you feel satiated (but not stuffed). Here are a few of my go-tos that I always have on hand.

Basmati rice

Cassava flour (Bob's Red Mill)

Glutinous rice flour (Koda Farms)*

Jasmine rice

Rice flour (Erawan or Bob's Red Mill)*

Spring roll wrappers (8 in [20 cm] Spring Home TYJ Spring Roll Pastry)

Sweet potato noodles

*Rice flour has a finer texture than glutinous rice flour and is often used as a wheat flour substitute in gluten-free baking or for thickening sauces. Glutinous rice flour has a stickier and denser texture. It is commonly used in Asian desserts and dishes that require a chewy or sticky texture, such as mochi, dumplings, rice cakes, and bibingka.

Sawsawan

Sauces, Condiments, Pickles, and Pantry Items

Sawsawan, in English, means "sauce," and sauces, dressings, toppings, and marinades are an integral part of not just Filipino food but my overall approach to cooking. I love sauces and dressings almost more than the meals themselves. At the very least, they can be the small touches that really bring everything together and make it sing.

One way to make a meal special is to make all these sauces and toppings from scratch instead of buying premade or bottled versions at the store. (It's what makes restaurant meals stand out!) This chapter includes a few of my favorite and most versatile sauce recipes—many of which you can make, store in the fridge, and have on hand for whenever you're putting together a special meal for friends or even just yourself.

Coconut Labneh

This sauce is inspired by the traditional Greek yogurt cheese known as labneh. I really love and respect the Middle Eastern way of eating and cooking, so it was fun for me to take a classic Middle Eastern recipe and make it my own. My big twist, as it were, is to use coconut yogurt and strain it until it becomes thick, creamy, and cloudlike—that really robust, whipped texture just brings a smile to my face. I always like to have a bit of this labneh on hand because it really elevates a humdrum recipe at a moment's notice. Just plop a dollop on a plate, toss some roasted veggies on top, and it magically becomes like a proper restaurant-level dish—suddenly, the plate looks alluring and artistic! You're a chef, baby! Even roasted vegetables, which are admittedly delicious but can be not-so-pretty, look eleganza mama when served on a cloud of coconut labneh.

MAKES 2 CUPS [455 G]

2 cups [455 g] coconut yogurt

1 tsp kosher salt

Juice of 1 lemon

Place a fine-mesh sieve in a medium bowl. Make sure there's enough space between the bottom of the sieve and the base of the bowl for the liquid to release. Lay a double layer of cheesecloth in the sieve.

In a separate medium bowl, stir together the coconut yogurt, salt, and lemon juice. Transfer the yogurt to the cheesecloth-lined sieve. Carefully bring the edges of the cheesecloth together and tie it in a knot. Let the bowl sit in the refrigerator overnight or for up to 24 hours to achieve a thick labneh consistency.

Transfer the labneh to an airtight container and refrigerate for up to 2 weeks.

Coconut Green Goddess Dressing

This is my spin on green goddess dressing, which is such a go-to for so many occasions. Usually the base is mayonnaise or yogurt, but I make it with coconut yogurt. Not only does it give it a slightly island-y vibe, but it also makes it a vegan treat. Then I add in a ton of herbs, jalapeño, and lime juice to brighten it and amp up the herby, earthy flavors.

This sauce is quite adaptable. It can be a thinner, dressing-like consistency when you first make it (sometimes I'll even just drizzle it on some simple steamed rice!), but if you put it in the fridge for a few days, it thickens up enough to use as a schmear on a sandwich or as a swoosh of yumminess beneath a platter of roasted vegetables. I made this for a private chef client recently, and they lost their minds, which just reminded me how good this is.

MAKES APPROXIMATELY 1¾ CUPS [420 G]

1 cup [20 g] cilantro leaves and tender stems

1 cup [20 g] Italian parsley leaves

1 jalapeño, stemmed

2 garlic cloves

Juice of 2 limes

½ cup [120 g] coconut yogurt

½ cup [120 ml] avocado or canola oil

2 tsp kosher salt

In the jar of a blender, blend all the ingredients together until smooth and the mixture turns a bright green color. Transfer to an airtight container and refrigerate for up to 7 days.

Coconut Hot Sauce

When you go to the Philippines, there are palm trees everywhere. I sometimes take for granted that coconut is just one of those base flavors that was part of my life growing up; it's a common flavor in Southeast Asian cooking in general. I'm always trying to think of new and interesting ways it could be used in cooking. So, hello Coconut Hot Sauce!

This sauce is bright and beautiful, an orangey-red, sweet, and spicy treat. If I were to have a hot sauce line, this would be my first product (call me, Cholula!). It's great for anytime you want a little heat or spice; it's a perfect dipping sauce for crudités, lumpia, chips—all that snacky stuff. It's a tad thicker than your traditional hot sauce, and I love the way it coats food and then drips down your throat—sensual! Seriously, this is unlike anything I've ever seen in a store (Cholula, seriously, call me). If you are not a spicy person, make sure to take out the chile seeds, but if you want to live dangerously, leave 'em in.

MAKES 1¾ CUPS [430 ML]

9 Fresno chiles

5 garlic cloves

3 Tbsp white vinegar

¼ cup [60 ml] sweet chili sauce

¼ cup [60 ml] full-fat unsweetened coconut milk

1 Tbsp sugar

¼ cup [60 ml] melted unrefined coconut oil

Kosher salt

In a medium saucepan over medium heat, bring 6 cups [1.4 L] of water to a boil. Add the chiles and garlic and cook for 3 minutes, or until the chiles turn bright red. Using a slotted spoon, carefully transfer the chiles and garlic to the jar of a blender. Add the vinegar, sweet chili sauce, coconut milk, and sugar and blend until smooth. Stream in the melted coconut oil while blending on low speed, then increase the speed to high and blend until completely smooth. Season with salt to taste. Transfer to an airtight container and refrigerate for up to 2 weeks.

Chili Paste

This is similar to a classic sambal oelek, a spicy chili paste that you can easily find at a bodega or Asian market. However, I will tell you a secret: One way to show off and make your food taste just that much better is to make this common little chili paste yourself. Like making your own green goddess dressing or hot sauce, a chili paste from scratch is an easy-breezy way to blow your guests' socks off. It elevates your dishes and impresses your friends; what's not to love? And as the Spice Girls once wisely said, spice up your life!

MAKES 1 CUP [220 G]

5 Fresno chiles, stemmed and chopped, or 80 Thai chiles, stemmed

1 garlic clove

⅓ cup [80 ml] rice vinegar

2 Tbsp sugar

1 tsp kosher salt, plus more to taste

In a food processor, blend all the ingredients until the chiles form a paste and the mixture becomes slightly liquefied. Beware that the spice from the chiles is quite hot and can cause coughing if inhaled. Carefully taste and season with more salt to your liking. Transfer to an airtight container or jar and refrigerate for up to 2 weeks.

Sweet and Spicy Banana Ketchup

Banana ketchup is a Filipino staple, our version of (you guessed it!) ketchup. I remember eating it with egg rolls growing up, but it's kind of just everywhere, paired with everything. It's more nuanced and layered than American ketchup (sorry), with the sweetness of bananas, the kick of spices, and the sharp tang of vinegar. While you can find this condiment in stores and online, and it's usable as is, I like to add a few more things to it—like cumin for an unexpected, almost arid, element. Use this ketchup as a glaze, sauce, or marinade for vegetables or proteins. Feel free to double the recipe if you want a bigger portion. It's an amazing condiment that gets a lot of use, something you're always happy to have in the fridge.

MAKES ½ CUP [ABOUT 120 G]

¼ cup [60 g] banana ketchup

2 Tbsp tamari

2 Tbsp Chili Paste (page 45, or store-bought)

2 Tbsp unseasoned rice vinegar

1 Tbsp avocado or canola oil

1 Tbsp sesame oil

1 Tbsp maple syrup

1 tsp ground cumin

In a medium bowl, whisk together all the ingredients until combined. Transfer to an airtight container and refrigerate for up to 7 days.

Herby Fish Sauce

This is my Filipino-ish version of a salsa verde with a bit of a funky-fishy-salty-fermented profile. Don't let the fish sauce scare you! You don't really taste it here, but it adds this deep, layered, salty, oceanic, umami profile that is really enticing. The best way I can describe it is that the sauce feels like it's of the ocean, if that makes sense. Anchovies add a beautiful, robust, warm flavor that salt on its own can't provide.

MAKES 1½ CUPS [370 ML]

2 poblano chiles

½ cup [120 ml] sweet chili sauce

¼ cup [60 ml] fish sauce

¼ cup [5 g] Italian parsley, roughly chopped

¼ cup [5 g] cilantro, roughly chopped

3 green onions, chopped

1 jalapeño, seeded and chopped

Zest and juice of 4 limes

Kosher salt

Freshly ground black pepper

Preheat the oven on to 400°F [200°C]. Line a baking sheet with aluminum foil.

Place the peppers on the baking sheet and roast for 30 minutes, flipping them a couple of times, until the skins get crinkled and blackened.

Transfer the chiles to a medium bowl and cover the top of the bowl with plastic. This will allow the skin to steam and make it easier to remove. Let the peppers cool for 10 minutes.

Using your hands, gently peel away and discard the skin. Remove and discard the seeds. Roughly chop the chiles into small, chunky pieces and set aside.

In a clean medium bowl, add the sweet chili sauce, fish sauce, parsley, cilantro, green onions, jalapeño, lime zest, and lime juice. Stir until well combined. Stir in the chiles and season with salt and pepper to taste. Transfer to an airtight container and refrigerate for up to 7 days.

Peanut Salsa

As you know by now, I love a sauce—truly, this whole chapter is my ode to toppings! And this one just might be my favorite, though that's a little like picking a favorite child. However, this chunky and flavor-packed sauce does have all my favorite components: She's crunchy, she's acidic, she's spicy, she's herby, she's fatty. She's got it all.

I call this a salsa because I've taken the idea of a salsa macha but used ingredients you'd find in a Filipino-ish pantry, in this case, my pantry. I put this on noodles, roasted potatoes, or toast with whipped tofu or cottage cheese. Honestly, I can't think of a single thing that it wouldn't make better!

Also, side note to my peanut allergy girlies: I love you, and if you really want this in your repertoire (and who could blame you?) you could sub in cashews, which are a bit fattier and, honestly, my favorite nut! (Peanuts are also my favorite but they are technically legumes, so I get a pass there.) Anyway, make a big old bowl of this and have it in the fridge at all times. She's the perfect topper for anything that comes your way.

MAKES ABOUT 1 CUP [220 G]

¼ cup [30 g] chopped toasted unsalted peanuts

3 green onions, green and white parts, finely chopped

1 jalapeño, finely chopped

2 garlic cloves, finely chopped

¼ cup [60 ml] sweet chili sauce

Zest and juice of 2 limes

¼ tsp kosher salt

¼ tsp freshly ground black pepper

In a medium bowl, combine the peanuts, green onions, jalapeño, garlic, sweet chili sauce, lime zest, and lime juice. Mix well and season with the salt and pepper. Transfer to an airtight container and refrigerate for up to 7 days.

Whipped Tahini (or I Can't Believe It's Not Cheese!)

The wacky thing about this whipped delight is that it tastes just like cheddar cheese! It's fluffy, creamy, and so, so cheesy (in a good way, not a "dad joke" way). I definitely did not set out to create a cheese replacement when I was toying around with miso and tahini, but I'm not mad that I stumbled upon it, especially because it has so many uses. Schmear it on a plate that you then pile high with salad, or try it as a sauce for dipping anything from vegetable crudités to lumpia. My big tip is to make sure to really blend this well, because aerating it and giving it that really whipped, cloudlike texture is key.

MAKES 1½ CUPS [360 G]

1 cup [220 g] tahini

⅓ cup [80 ml] unseasoned rice vinegar

¼ cup [60 g] reduced sodium miso paste

½ cup [120 ml] cold water

2 tsp kosher salt

In a food processor, combine the tahini, rice vinegar, and miso. Pulse until the mixture is fully combined. Stream in some of the cold water with the motor running. Stop the food processor and, using a rubber spatula, scrape down the sides and season with the salt. Pulse the mixture again and stream in the remaining water slowly. Let it blend for about 5 minutes until the mixture whips into a cloudy and creamy texture. Give your whipped tahini a taste and season with more salt to taste. Transfer the whipped tahini to an airtight container and refrigerate for up to 7 days.

Honey Lime Vinaigrette

Let's level up the vinaigrette game with this puckery and flavorful dressing infused with a hint of patis, a.k.a. fish sauce! The combo of sweet honey, zesty lime, and savory fish sauce creates a harmonious balance of flavors that pairs deliciously with fresh greens or grilled vegetables. I also like to toss it on my Ensaladang Peach (page 188) in the summer.

MAKES 1¼ CUPS [310 ML]

½ cup [120 ml] extra-virgin olive oil

¼ cup [60 ml] fresh lime juice
    (from about 2 limes)

2 Tbsp honey

1½ Tbsp fish sauce

1 small shallot, finely chopped

1 small jalapeño, seeded and finely chopped

Freshly ground black pepper

In a large bowl, mix together the olive oil, lime juice, honey, fish sauce, shallot, jalapeño, and black pepper. Store in an airtight container in the refrigerator for up to 7 days.

Adobo Vinaigrette

This is a version of the classic adobo sauce, but conceived more as a salad dressing than a traditional sauce. Still, it packs that tangy, salty, spicy combination of flavors that is the essence of adobo.

MAKES ½ CUP [120 ML]

¼ cup [60 ml] extra-virgin olive oil

2 Tbsp white vinegar

2 Tbsp tamari

3 garlic cloves, grated

1 Tbsp sugar

1 tsp chili flakes

1 tsp kosher salt

In a small bowl, whisk together the olive oil, vinegar, tamari, garlic, sugar, chili flakes, and salt until combined. Transfer to an airtight container and refrigerate for up to 7 days.

Vinegar Sauce

In traditional Filipino cooking, anything that's grilled or fried is served with a vinegar sauce, as it really cuts through and balances the fatty, unctuous flavor. It's there to act as a counterbalance and brighten the dish, to make it feel complete and not too heavy-handed. (It's like how on *The Great British Bake Off* they always want something tart to balance the sweet.) This is the sharp, tangy zing that so many decadent meals need. It's very much the little oomph that makes the whole meal sing and brings all the flavors together. When I was a kid, I loved it so much that I would ask my mom for a shot of it! I would literally drink it! I think you may find yourself liking it that much too.

MAKES ¾ CUP [180 ML]

¾ cup [180 ml] cane vinegar

3 Tbsp sugar

1 Thai chile, sliced crosswise

2 garlic cloves, minced

1 Tbsp minced chives

In a small bowl, stir together the vinegar, sugar, chile, garlic, and chives until combined. Transfer to an airtight container and refrigerate for up to 7 days.

Pancit Dressing

Pancit is Filipino stir-fried noodles, a pretty simple dish, which means the sauce is key. Don't worry, I've got an amazing one, of course! What makes this one so special is that it really encapsulates all the flavors I grew up with, or what I call the Big Five *S*'s: sweet, spicy, salty, and sour, to start. And the fifth? Sesame seed oil! Although technically not a flavor, the sesame oil may just be the most important *S*. It just adds this slippery, nutty *mmmmmm* to finish it off.

This dressing obviously pairs really well with noodles, but I also love using it on a salad or as a marinade. It's just a no-fuss flavor bomb. And it's especially great as a finishing sauce—a little drizzle right before you drop the food on the table, that happy ending every dish needs.

MAKES 2 CUPS [480 ML]

½ cup [120 ml] sweet chili sauce

¼ cup [60 ml] rice vinegar

3 Tbsp tamari

2 Tbsp Chili Paste (page 45, or store-bought)

2 Tbsp sesame oil

¾ cup [180 ml] neutral oil, such as canola or grapeseed oil

2 garlic cloves, minced

One 3 in [7.5 cm] piece fresh ginger, peeled and grated

Kosher salt

Freshly ground black pepper

In a medium mixing bowl, whisk together the sweet chili sauce, rice vinegar, tamari, chili paste, sesame oil, neutral oil, garlic, and ginger. Season with salt and pepper to taste. Transfer to an airtight container and refrigerate for up to 2 weeks.

Spicy Miso Tahini

This creamy, dreamy sauce is a mix of Middle Eastern and Southeast Asian flavors. The tahini has a rich, unctuous, velvety consistency but—surprise!—there's no cream in it. Then add that umami miso and you have this luscious sauce with just a bit of tartness from the rice vinegar and heat from the ginger and chili paste. A real symphony of flavors. It goes a long way, too: a marinade, a salad dressing, a dip for vegetables, you name it.

MAKES 1¼ CUPS [310 ML]

⅓ cup [75 g] tahini

2 Tbsp reduced sodium miso paste

3 Tbsp sweet chili sauce

3 Tbsp rice vinegar

3 Tbsp tamari

3 Tbsp sesame oil

2 Tbsp Chili Paste (page 45, or store-bought)

2 garlic cloves, grated

One 3 in [7.5 cm] piece fresh ginger, peeled and grated

Kosher salt

Freshly ground black pepper

In a medium bowl, add the tahini, miso, sweet chili sauce, rice vinegar, tamari, sesame oil, chili paste, garlic, ginger, and ¼ cup [60 ml] of warm water. Whisk together until combined. Season with salt and pepper to taste. Transfer to an airtight container and refrigerate for up to 7 days.

Miso Mushroom Bagoong

A word about bagoong. First of all, it's pronounced bag-ah-oooooong: three syllables and a bit of a drag on that last one. It's a traditional Filipino condiment, usually made from shrimp paste, which gives it a really umami, salty, briny, even funky (in the best possible way) taste. This bagoong was inspired by a sauce by my friend Andrea Gentl—a mushroom bagna cauda (which literally means "hot bath"). It's made with porcini mushroom powder, tons of garlic, and red miso to achieve that pasty, funky flavor of a traditional bagoong. It's best paired with fresh fruit or vegetables to add some surprising, rich character to an otherwise straightforward ingredient.

MAKES 3 CUPS [720 ML]

2 cups [480 ml] extra-virgin olive oil

20 garlic cloves, smashed

¼ cup [35 g] porcini powder

2 Tbsp chili flakes

¼ cup [70 g] organic red miso (hikari haccho, a.k.a. red miso paste)

2 Tbsp tamari

2 Tbsp coconut jam (pika pika) or maple syrup

In a medium saucepan over low heat, add the olive oil and garlic. Cook low and slow, stirring often, for 10 minutes, or until the garlic is soft and caramelized. Add the porcini powder and chili flakes. Carefully whisk in the miso until it completely melts in the oil. Let it cook for an additional 3 minutes. Using a wooden spoon, mash the garlic into the oil.

Turn off the heat and whisk in the tamari and coconut jam until combined, about 45 seconds. Let the mixture cool to room temperature so the flavors harmonize. Transfer the solids to a blender, reserving the oil. Blend until smooth, gradually streaming in the reserved oil. Use a rubber spatula as needed to mix and ensure it gets blended and emulsified.

Transfer to a saucepan over low heat and serve right away.

Mushroom BBQ Sauce

Indulge in the vibrant flavors of a Filipino-ish summer with this Mushroom BBQ Sauce! This BBQ sauce is a riff on a marinade my mom used to make. The layered flavor—umami, vinegary, spicy, and sweet—is very versatile. Try it with the mushroom skewers on page 200 or with noodles, salads, grilled vegetables—anything that could use a little oomph in the flavor department. This fusion of flavors will transport you to sun-soaked barbecues and vibey gatherings!

MAKES 1¾ CUPS [440 ML]

¾ cup [180 ml] neutral oil, such as canola or grapeseed oil

¼ cup [60 ml] mushroom soy sauce

¼ cup [60 ml] Sweet and Spicy Banana Ketchup (page 49, or store-bought)

¼ cup [60 ml] sweet chili sauce

¼ cup [60 ml] white vinegar

5 garlic cloves

One 1 in [2.5 cm] piece fresh ginger, peeled

In a medium bowl, whisk together the oil, mushroom soy sauce, banana ketchup, sweet chili sauce, and white vinegar. Grate the garlic and ginger into the sauce and whisk vigorously. If you can't help yourself from tasting the sauce, I'll allow you to dip your index finger in it now (you're welcome)! Transfer to an airtight container and refrigerate for up to 7 days.

Ginger Sauce

When I was a kid, ginger sauce was this all-purpose sticky brown sauce that came in a bottle. It's usually made with pork liver to give it its richness and flavor. But pork liver is difficult to find and a bit heavy, so I came up with a lighter, easier version of this traditional Filipino sauce and, to be honest, I think it's just as good. It is a bit time-consuming, though, because you have to roast the ginger for a really long time to get it all shriveled and concentrate the flavor, but it's worth it. Then you blend it with tamari, lime, and sweet chili sauce and it makes this thick, savory, tangy, bright, and warming sauce that has layers and layers of competing and complementary flavors. The seasonings make it perfect for cooler times of year. But, to be honest, it's great year-round.

MAKES ABOUT 5 CUPS [1.2 L]

1 lb [455 g] fresh ginger, peeled

6 garlic cloves

1 cup [240 ml] tamari

2 cups [480 ml] sweet chili sauce

½ cup [120 ml] fresh lime juice

½ cup [120 ml] sesame oil

¼ cup [55 g] Chili Paste (page 45, or store-bought)

Kosher salt

Freshly ground black pepper

Preheat the oven to 350°F [180°C]. Line a baking sheet with parchment paper.

Scatter the ginger out evenly on the baking sheet. Roast the ginger for 1 hour. Let cool for 10 minutes.

To the jar of a blender, add the roasted ginger, garlic, tamari, sweet chili sauce, lime juice, sesame oil, and chili paste and blend until smooth. Add 2 to 3 Tbsp of warm water and blend again. Season with salt and pepper to taste. Transfer to an airtight container and refrigerate for up to 2 weeks.

Sawsawan

Creamy Whipped Tofu

My editors were like, Woldy, another dip!? And to that I said: YES. I love a dip, I always crave a dip, give me a dip and I'm happy. This one I love because it's fully vegan. Wonderful whipped tofu gets some earthy miso and a dash of sharp, acidic vinegar. The result is similar to coconut labneh in texture—velvety, spreadable, creamy, dreamy. And it's oh-so-YUM. Serve it with raw or pickled vegetables or chips or crackers and watch it disappear. Also watch everyone's jaws drop when you tell them it's fully vegan!

MAKES 1¼ CUPS [390 G]

One 14 oz [400 g] block firm tofu, patted dry with a paper towel

1 garlic clove

2 Tbsp rice vinegar

1 Tbsp miso paste

1 tsp kosher salt

2 Tbsp extra-virgin avocado oil

Using your hands, crumble the tofu into small, chunky pieces into the bowl of a food processor. Using a Microplane, grate the garlic in with the tofu. Add the rice vinegar and miso and season with the salt. Blend until smooth, 3 to 5 minutes. While it's blending, stream in the avocado oil. Transfer the whipped tofu to an airtight container and refrigerate for up to 2 weeks.

Seedy Chili Oil

I think crunch and heat are probably the most underrated texture and flavor, respectively. And this chili oil brings the two together in such a fun, dynamic way. The mix of spicy, smoky, and seedy makes this a really bold finishing sauce that adds a lot of life and excitement to every dish it comes in contact with. It sort of dances in your mouth. I highly suggest making a bunch, keeping it in an airtight container in the fridge, and spooning a generous helping on top of any dish that needs an extra little oomph.

MAKES ABOUT 5¼ CUPS [1.25 L]

½ cup [50 g] dried hathei chili powder (Diaspora) or red pepper flakes

½ cup [75 g] pumpkin seeds

½ cup [35 g] fried shallots (Maesri)

¼ cup [30 g] sesame seeds

1 tsp kosher salt

2 cups [480 ml] neutral oil, such as grapeseed or canola oil

3 Tbsp sesame oil

1 Tbsp maple syrup

2 tsp white vinegar

In a large glass jar with an airtight lid, add the chili powder, pumpkin seeds, fried shallots, sesame seeds, and salt.

In a medium saucepan over medium heat, warm the neutral oil for about 5 minutes.

Gently pour the hot oil over the chili-seed mixture and let it sizzle and dance. Stir with a metal spoon, then add the sesame oil, maple syrup, and vinegar. Stir to combine, then let cool completely.

Store with the airtight lid in the refrigerator for up to 1 month and bring her out whenever you're ready to play.

Sweet Buttered Nuts

Five ingredients that, together, will change your life. You start with pistachios bathed in butter. Wait for the deliciously nutty aroma, then throw in some spice, salt, and sweetness, and voilà! Divine nuts living in a pool of fatty goodness. Who doesn't want that?

MAKES 1 CUP [255 G]

½ cup [115 g] unsalted butter

1 cup [140 g] raw shelled pistachios

2 Tbsp dark maple syrup

2 tsp kosher salt

1 tsp chili flakes

In a small saucepan over medium-low heat, melt the butter. Once the butter is melted, immediately add the pistachios. Let the pistachios bathe in the butter, swirling occasionally, until the nuts are toasty, the butter is foamy, and you can smell a nutty aroma, about 6 minutes. Stand in front of the stove and watch the butter and nuts super closely so they don't burn! Swirl the pan a few more times, then remove the saucepan from the heat and carefully splash in the maple syrup. The syrup might pop off and the butter might bubble to the top for a couple of seconds, so be careful. Add the salt and chili flakes. Give the pan a couple more swirls and, using a rubber spatula, stir to combine. Serve immediately over your desired dish, or store the cooled nuts in an airtight glass jar in the refrigerator for up to 2 weeks. When ready to use, reheat the buttered nuts in a small pan until the butter is completely melted.

Easy Crispy Garlic

This is a very important ingredient in my cooking— just roughly chopped garlic fried in oil. It is a perfect little bit of flavorful crunch to top a salad, a soup, or some roasted vegetables. I love that you get both the garlic crumbles themselves and then the flavored garlic oil, which you can also use for marinades or as a finishing drizzle. Like, do I sometimes buy those store-bought garlic crunches that are sold at Asian markets or even bigger chains? Yes, totally. But when I have the time and energy (and lots of garlic that could go bad), I make it myself, and I always remember that it tastes way better homemade. Such is life!

MAKES ½ CUP [25 G] CRISPY GARLIC AND 1 CUP [240 ML] OIL

1 cup [240 ml] neutral oil, such as canola or grapeseed oil

1 head garlic, cloves peeled and chopped, or 20 garlic cloves

1 tsp kosher salt

In a medium saucepan, add the oil and chopped garlic. Set over medium-low heat and attentively watch the garlic fry until it becomes golden brown, 3 to 5 minutes. To prevent the garlic from burning, gently swirl the saucepan from time to time.

As soon as the garlic is golden brown and crispy, use a slotted spoon to remove the garlic chips and transfer to a paper towel–lined plate. Let the garlic drain. Season with salt and let cool completely. Use immediately or store in an airtight container in a cool, dark place for up to 7 days.

Transfer the cooled garlic oil to a separate airtight container and store in a cool, dark place for up to 2 weeks. Use the oil in vinaigrettes, sauces, or dips.

Seedy Coconut Confetti

When I finish off a dish, I love to have something that's crunchy and flavorful. You always want more flavor, layers and layers of it. This crumble is the perfect thing to sprinkle on top of a soup, salad, or protein for added crunch, but also for the tropical and coconutty flavor. She's a crunchy top, and we love her for it.

MAKES ABOUT 1 CUP [150 G]

½ cup [40 g] unsweetened shredded coconut flakes

½ cup [70 g] raw pumpkin seeds

2 Tbsp black sesame seeds

3 dried makrut lime leaves

2 tsp chili flakes

1 tsp kosher salt

1 tsp sugar

In a medium frying pan over medium heat, toast the coconut flakes, pumpkin seeds, and sesame seeds for about 5 minutes until you start to smell their aromas. Be careful not to burn them. Using your hands, crush up the makrut lime leaves into the seed mixture. Remove from the heat and season with the chili flakes, salt, and sugar. Stir to combine. Let the mixture cool and stir again. Transfer to an airtight glass jar and store in a cool, dark place for up to 1 month.

Almond Goldenberry Gremolata

This gremolata is a showstopper. She brings texture, she brings flavor, she has everything you want: herby notes, brightness, punch, crunch, a vibrant green color. In my book, she can do no wrong.

MAKES ABOUT 1½ CUPS [300 G]

Zest and juice of 1 lemon

¼ cup [60 ml] rice vinegar

2 tsp fish sauce

½ cup [10 g] chopped parsley

1 Thai chile, thinly sliced

¾ cup [70 g] slivered almonds, toasted

¼ cup [40 g] dried goldenberries

1 tsp sugar

½ cup [120 ml] extra-virgin olive oil

Add all the ingredients to a small bowl and stir to combine. Give her a taste—you're looking for herbaceous and tangy. Transfer to an airtight container and refrigerate for up to 3 days.

Golden Raisin Gremolata

I'm a cilantro lover, and this gremolata lets me add cilantro to most any dish! Combined with pickled golden raisins, this topping adds buoyancy to braised and grilled dishes with its brightness and chewy texture. If you don't love cilantro, this recipe isn't for you. Just kidding! Swap the cilantro for any green herb—parsley, mint, or dill would be equally delicious.

MAKES ¼ CUP [50 G]

2 Tbsp Pickled Golden Raisins (page 62)

1 cup [20 g] chopped cilantro leaves

Zest and juice of 1 lime

1 jalapeño, seeded and chopped

2 garlic cloves, minced

In a small bowl, mix together the pickled golden raisins, cilantro, lime zest, lime juice, jalapeño, and garlic. Store in an airtight container and refrigerate for up to 3 days.

Rose Goldenberries

A delightful blend of floral, tart, and sweet. That is the best way to describe these deliciously juicy morsels. As the dried goldenberries soak in a syrup infused with floral notes, they plump up and undergo a delicious transformation. Serve them effortlessly over yogurt, alongside a slice of bibingka, or as a topping on ice cream for a delectable dessert!

MAKES 2¾ CUPS [650 G]

1½ cups [230 g] dried goldenberries

1 cup [200 g] granulated sugar

1 Tbsp edible dried rose petals

2 Tbsp rose water

In an airtight glass jar or 32 oz [960 ml] container, add the goldenberries. Set aside.

In a small saucepan over medium-low heat, add 1 cup [240 ml] of water along with the sugar and dried rose petals. Bring to a low simmer and use a rubber spatula to stir the mixture until the sugar has completely dissolved, 3 to 5 minutes.

Carefully pour the warm syrup into the container with the dried goldenberries. Let it cool at room temperature for 45 minutes to 1 hour, until the goldenberries plump up. Once cool, splash in the rose water and stir to combine. Cover and refrigerate the mixture for 24 hours to soak up the rose water essence before serving. Store the goldenberries in the airtight glass jar in the refrigerator for up to 2 weeks.

Pickled Golden Raisins

When I was little, it seemed like every dish my family served had raisins in it . . . and I hated it. Like . . . why?! Everything doesn't need raisins! But with age comes wisdom, and now I get it—raisins are these unexpected, juicy pearls of sweetness and moisture. They help add just that perfect bit of surprise and delight to a dish. How could I ever have doubted my family?! Ah, youth.

So this is my way of reclaiming this thing that I once didn't like and reimagining it for my adult life. I pickle the raisins in a zesty vinegar brine with the spicy heat of pink peppercorns and a dash of candied goodness from the sugar, and bam! They are such an amazing addition to basically any dish. A pot of herby rice? A salad that could use a little extra oomph? A sweet rice porridge or some hearty roast vegetables? All could benefit from some pickled raisins! These little guys add a burst of tangy-tart, juicy, honeyed beauty that will elevate everything. Trust me, these are game changers.

MAKES 2 CUPS [560 G]

1½ cups [235 g] golden raisins

1 cup [240 ml] cane vinegar

¼ cup [55 g] granulated sugar

2 Tbsp kosher salt

1 Tbsp pink peppercorns

1 tsp whole coriander seeds

To a clean, airtight glass jar, add the raisins.

In a medium saucepan over medium-low heat, combine the vinegar, sugar, salt, pink peppercorns, and coriander seeds with ½ cup [120 ml] of water. Bring to a simmer, stirring occasionally, until the sugar is dissolved, 1 to 2 minutes.

Carefully pour the liquid over the raisins, then let cool completely. Store with the lid on in the refrigerator for up to 3 months.

Pickled Bitter Melon

OK, I have a confession. I hated bitter melon as a kid! My lola grew it in her backyard. When she served it to me with beef and egg, I was bitter that I had to eat it! I'd pick around it in silent protest.

Fast-forward to today, and I decided to use bitter melon as an exercise in turning something that I hate eating into something I love eating. Pickling was the solution. By brining the melon—with vinegar and sugar and then throwing in chewy golden raisins and spicing it up with pink peppercorns, garlic, and chiles—it blossoms into this punchy, sweet condiment that can be scattered on salads or served alongside hearty, rich entrées like grilled or braised dishes.

MAKES 2 CUPS [200 G]

1 bitter melon (about 8 oz [230 g])

3 Thai chiles

2 garlic cloves

2 dried bay leaves

1 Tbsp whole coriander seeds

1 Tbsp pink peppercorns

2 cups [480 ml] cane vinegar

¼ cup [50 g] granulated sugar

1 tsp kosher salt

Cut off the ends of the bitter melon and discard. Cut the melon in half lengthwise. Using a metal spoon, scoop out and discard the white pith and seeds. Thinly slice the melon into half-moon shapes about ⅛ in [4 mm] thick. You should end up with 2 cups [200 g] of sliced bitter melon.

In a 32 oz [960 ml] clean glass Mason jar or deli container, add the bitter melon, chiles, garlic, bay leaves, coriander seeds, and pink peppercorns.

In a small pot, combine the vinegar, sugar, and salt with ½ cup [120 ml] of water. Simmer over medium heat until the sugar has dissolved.

Gently pour the brining liquid over the bitter melon in the jar. Let stand for 1 hour, or until it reaches room temperature. Cover the jar with the lid and refrigerate for up to 3 weeks.

Pickled Green Daikon

Raw green daikon is a peppery, crunchy little friend. Pickling it balances out some of those spicier notes with sweeter, earthier flavors. Add these on a sandwich, toss them in in a salad, or serve them with a yummy dip.

MAKES 2½ CUPS [380 G]

1 green daikon radish (about 12 oz [380 g])

3 Thai chiles

2 garlic cloves

2 bay leaves

1 Tbsp whole coriander seeds

1 Tbsp pink peppercorns

2 cups [480 ml] cane vinegar

¼ cup [50 g] sugar

1 tsp kosher salt

Using a sharp knife or mandoline, thinly slice the daikon into rounds about ⅛ in [4 mm] thick. You will end up with 2½ cups [380 g] of sliced daikon.

In a 32 oz [960 ml] clean glass jar or deli container, add the daikon, chiles, garlic, bay leaves, coriander seeds, and pink peppercorns.

In a small pot, combine the vinegar, sugar, and salt with ½ cup [120 ml] of water. Set over medium heat, bring to a simmer, and stir until the sugar has dissolved.

Gently pour the brining liquid into the jar. Let the mixture stand for 1 hour, or until it reaches room temperature. Cover the jar with the lid and refrigerate for up to 2 weeks.

Pickled Carrots

Girl, get that beta-carotene but make it spicy, spirited, and fun! My mom always told me carrots are good for your eyes, so this is my grown-up way of honoring her advice. Sophisticated, funky, with a little bit of crunch and heat, these pickled carrots can elevate a lot of different meals.

MAKES 1 QT [950 G]

1½ lb [680 g] small orange carrots, tops removed

3 Thai chiles

2 garlic cloves

2 bay leaves

1 Tbsp whole coriander seeds

1 Tbsp pink peppercorns

2 cups [480 ml] cane vinegar

¼ cup [50 g] sugar

1 tsp kosher salt

Cut the carrots lengthwise. In a 32 oz [960 ml] clean glass jar or deli container, add the carrots, chiles, garlic, bay leaves, coriander seeds, and pink peppercorns.

In a small pot, combine the vinegar, sugar, and salt with ½ cup [120 ml] of water. Set over medium heat, bring to a simmer, and stir until the sugar has dissolved.

Gently pour the brining liquid into the jar. Let the mixture stand for 1 hour, or until it reaches room temperature. Cover the jar with the lid and refrigerate for up to 2 weeks.

Shallot Confit

Confit is a French cooking technique that sounds très fancy but, in reality, is pretty straightforward. You just cook something low and slow in a fat—something like oil or butter. The method can be applied to many things, such as garlic or tomatoes, and it renders whatever you're cooking creamy and soft. Here I apply the technique to the sharp bite of shallots by cooking them in a really nice, bougie extra-virgin olive oil. I've added some of my favorite spices, such as bay leaf and whole black peppercorns, to infuse the oil and transfer those flavors to the shallots. The end result is this buttery, jammy shallot deliciousness with a slight undercurrent of heat and savoriness.

MAKES 3 CUPS [750 G]

1 lb [455 g] shallots (about 15 small shallots), peeled

1 Tbsp black peppercorns

3 bay leaves

2 cups [480 ml] extra-virgin olive oil

Preheat the oven to 350°F [180°C].

In an ovenproof dish, add the shallots, peppercorns, and bay leaves, then pour in the olive oil. Make sure the solids are completely submerged in the oil.

Cover the dish with aluminum foil and place on the middle rack of the oven. Bake for 1 hour or until the shallots transform into soft and luscious nuggets of goodness. Let cool completely.

Transfer the shallot confit and oil to an airtight container and store in the refrigerator for up to 2 weeks. To use, remove from the refrigerator and bring to room temperature, then serve immediately.

Quick Garlic Confit

For this confit, we cook the garlic in olive oil until it's so tender and soft it's like buttah, as Barbra Streisand would say. It becomes this creamy, rich, sweet flavor bomb. Because we cook it with bay leaves and pink peppercorns, there's a hint of savory flavoring in there, which just adds so much to it.

MAKES 1½ CUPS [515 G]

3 heads garlic, cloves peeled

2 bay leaves

1 Tbsp pink peppercorns

2 cups [480 ml] extra-virgin olive oil, plus more as needed

In a small oven-safe saucepan or cast-iron skillet, add the garlic cloves, bay leaves, pink peppercorns, and olive oil. Add more oil to make sure the garlic is completely submerged. Simmer over low heat for 30 minutes or until the garlic is soft and tender. Remove from the heat and let cool completely.

If not using the garlic right away, transfer the cloves to a glass jar and fill it up with the oil. Cover with the lid and refrigerate for up to 3 months.

Calamansi Marmalade

Calamansi is a citrus fruit that's a cross between a kumquat and a small lime. (It comes in two varieties; opt for the orange one, as it's softer and better for this particular recipe.) I love that calamansi—and all citrus—is in season during the winter; it's like nature knows you need a little burst of joy during the cold, gray months. I even know some people who grow small calamansi trees inside during the winter. When I was growing up, we had a calamansi tree in our backyard—it was gigantic and tall and watched over me my entire childhood. My mom would use the calamansi juice in sauces and marinades. I recently made this marmalade with her, which really concentrates and amplifies the fruit's tangy and tart energy into a sweet and yummy jam. She had never thought to make calamansi into a jam, but she loved it. Try it on a piece of sourdough bread. It's like a little smear of sunshine!

MAKES ABOUT 2 QT [1.9 KG]

4 lb [1.8 kg] calamansi, halved and seeded
8 cups [1.6 kg] sugar
Sliced and toasted sourdough bread, for serving
Flaky sea salt, for serving

In a medium pot over medium heat, add the calamansi, sugar, and 4 cups [960 ml] of water. Stir with a rubber spatula, then bring to a simmer. Decrease the heat to low and cook until golden and syrupy, stirring occasionally, about 2 hours and 40 minutes.

Remove from the heat and let the mixture cool completely.

Transfer the cooled calamansi marmalade to a container with a tight-fitting lid. Store in the refrigerator for up to 2 weeks.

To serve, spoon calamansi marmalade right onto the toast, sprinkle with flaky sea salt, and enjoy!

Calamansi Syrup

This recipe takes the bright tang of the calamansi fruit and concentrates its flavor into a sticky, decadent syrup. It's a thick and vibrant goo that perfectly balances sour and sweet. How could you not love it?

MAKES 1 CUP [240 ML]

1 cup [300 g] Calamansi Marmalade (at left)

In a small pot over medium heat, stir together the calamansi marmalade and ½ cup [120 ml] of water. Bring to a boil, then decrease the heat to low and simmer for 5 minutes. Remove from the heat and cool for 10 minutes.

Using a fine-mesh sieve set over a bowl, strain the syrup, using a rubber spatula to press down on the solids to get all the liquid gold. Transfer the syrup to a small jar with a tight-fitting lid. Refrigerate for up to 2 weeks.

Candied Kumquats

This is my ode to winter citrus! Kumquats may not be as juicy and bright as calamansi fruit, but they bring brightness to a gloomy day, especially when you candy and preserve them. Here you just toss them in a gloopy simple syrup to make tart, sugary little treats that are perfect as a topping. I like them on oatmeal, granola, cake, ice cream, Champorado (page 118), and so many things! Kumquats are only available for a short time in the winter, so take advantage of them while you can.

MAKES 2¼ CUPS [680 G]

2 cups [200 g] granulated sugar

2 cups [220 g] kumquats, sliced

In a medium saucepan over medium-low heat, combine the sugar with 1 cup [240 ml] of water. Using a rubber spatula, stir the mixture until the sugar has dissolved. Gently toss in the sliced kumquats and stir. Cook until golden and syrupy, about 25 minutes, stirring occasionally. Remove from the heat and let her cool completely.

Transfer the cooled kumquats to a container with a tight-fitting lid. Store in the refrigerator for up to 2 weeks.

Coconut Palm Sugar Syrup

This is a simple, sweet sauce perfect for drizzling on baked goods like Bibingka Pancakes (page 136) or some banana bread. The coconut palm sugar is less refined than traditional sugar, so it's, in theory, "healthier" or, at the very least, a less processed option, and adds just a hint of additional flavor. Coconut palm sugar and water, and bam! You've got an elegant, jazzy little drizzle for all your sweet-tooth needs!

MAKES 1½ CUPS [360 ML]

1 cup [190 g] coconut palm sugar

In a small saucepan over medium heat, combine the coconut palm sugar with 1 cup [240 ml] of water. Stir and bring to a low boil until the sugar dissolves and the syrup begins to thicken, 5 to 7 minutes. Dip a clean metal spoon into the syrup and check the back of the spoon; the syrup should completely cover the spoon and drip off slowly. Remove the syrup from the heat and let cool completely. Transfer to an airtight glass jar and store in the refrigerator for up to 1 month.

Coconut Yogurt Cream

This is inspired by something made by my friend Edouard Massih, the queer Lebanese chef of the bodega Edy's Grocer in Greenpoint, Brooklyn. At a collaborative pop-up dinner, I made a bibingka and he made an accompanying labneh mousse. I loved how creamy and pillowy it was. I thought about how it would be a perfect accompaniment to so many sweet dishes and how using coconut yogurt could add a bit of flair to it. Well, reader, I was right—this coconut yogurt cream is just so charming—creamy, rich, fluffy, like a little pile of tropical clouds. Put it on top of a cake, or toss some macerated fruit on it for a simple, delightful dish. You'll see this recipe used a few different ways throughout the book, but I encourage you to experiment with it on your own too.

MAKES 4 CUPS [480 G]

1 cup [240 ml] heavy whipping cream

2 Tbsp granulated sugar

1 tsp kosher salt

1 tsp vanilla extract

1 cup [240 g] coconut yogurt

To mix by hand, chill a medium metal mixing bowl in the freezer for 5 minutes. Add the heavy whipping cream, sugar, salt, and vanilla. With a wire whisk, beat the cream until soft peaks form, 4 to 5 minutes. Alternatively, you can do this in a stand mixer and whisk for 2 to 5 minutes, starting at low speed and gradually increasing to medium speed.

Using a rubber spatula, gently fold the coconut yogurt into the whipped cream until it is fully combined.

Transfer the coconut mousse to a large glass bowl and cover the bowl with plastic wrap. Chill in the refrigerator for at least 8 hours.

Serve immediately. Store in an airtight container or divide among individual serving dishes and cover each with plastic wrap for up to 1 day.

Winter

Family, Nostalgia, and a Warm Bowl of Rice Porridge

Winter is a season of decadence and indulgence. While lots of people really embrace autumn, winter is less beloved. It's easy to see why—she's gloomier, with shorter days filled with drab, cloudy, gray skies and unforgiving weather. And yet, don't be fooled—the season offers up some magical delights if you look for them hard enough.

I take these chilly months as a time to luxuriate in self-care and get cozy. It's a time of rest and renewal, of hibernating, of making plans and dreaming. It's nature's way of reminding you that you can't always be go-go-go, that rest is a crucial part of life's cycle, and that only after some downtime can you feel ready to take on the world. As such, you'll catch me reading a book (preferably by a fire), bingeing a TV show (preferably involving fighting Housewives), and napping (preferably midafternoon).

From a food perspective, this time of year brings to mind dishes that are warming, versatile, easy to make, soothing, and soulful. The first thing I think of is a gloopy rice porridge—most Asian countries have some version of this, and Filipinos are no different. It's something you can put in a pot and have bubbling away all day, a no-fuss meal that is endlessly customizable. Take a big scoop of that thick, creamy stew, drop it into a bowl, and dress it with whatever you have handy—hearty vegetables, aromatic alliums, or some condiments like my Seedy Chili Oil (page 56) or Miso Mushroom Bagoong (page 54). Mix in some spices like the full-bodied heat of ginger or the spicy zing of fried garlic, and let it warm you from the inside out. Having that grounding, velvety bowl of goodness while the world outside is so cold will make you feel safe and cared for, which is all anyone can ask for.

Winter is also a time when we get to embrace the potatoes, and dense, protein-rich beans. This is a time to really explore earthy, hearty flavors and creamy, velvety textures. It's a time to fill your belly and be restful and reflective. Winter lets us embrace bitter greens and hearty root vegetables, ingredients I've come to appreciate living in upstate New York. Surprisingly, there are many salads in this chapter, featuring the bite of radicchio or radish and herb salad with warm, sweet buttered nuts. We need greens even in winter! This chapter also includes stews with winter squashes, potatoes, and protein-rich beans, showcasing earthy, hearty flavors and creamy textures.

Because I think of seeking warmth in the winter, I think of my family, and the comfort of nostalgia and fond memories. As a Filipino American who grew up in Southern California, my childhood wasn't filled with cold winters—in fact, quite the opposite. I remember going to the Philippines with my family in December, and it would be borderline hot! It's there that I got a glimpse of my own history as my grandmother reunited with her extended family and showed us the humble home where she raised our mom and nine people slept in one room. I was amazed and proud of how far she had come and how hard she had worked to provide a better life for her children and for me. My father died when I was a teenager, which was a really difficult time and changed my family forever. It rocked my world. But my mother and grandmother were there to ensure that we felt bonded and connected to one another and always had support and love surrounding us. And so many times, that love was expressed through food.

It's that tender glow of family that helps get me through the winters, which can be lonely, especially for a single person. As a chef, making foods that remind me of home help me feel connected to my loved ones, who are so far away. Maybe it's a vegetable lumpia like my lola used to make, or a warm kale laing, which is my salad version of a traditional dish that's akin to creamed spinach. Or mung beans cooked in sumptuous coconut milk. These recipes are healing to me and remind me of what it was like to be a kid, looking at the world with wonder.

I hope these dishes help you embrace winter's charm. Invite your "chosen family," wrap up in blankets, and enjoy a classic movie or gossip about the *Real Housewives* around a table with a big Staub pot in the middle. Sip wine or hot tea, and savor the coziness of the season. You deserve the break.

Stovetop Jasmine Rice

MAKES 6 CUPS [1.2 KG] COOKED RICE, ABOUT 4 SERVINGS

2 cups [400 g] uncooked jasmine rice

1 tsp kosher salt

Anyone who has lived in or visited a Filipino household knows that it's not complete without a rice cooker filled with steaming hot rice in the kitchen! It's truly as essential as having a couch in the living room or a bed in the bedroom (or a karaoke machine in the dining room). In other words, an absolute nonnegotiable. However, if you don't have a rice cooker, I will refrain from judging you too hard. Instead, I'll give you a solution—an easy, breezy jasmine rice recipe to whip up at a moment's notice on the stove.

What I love about jasmine rice is that it's a classic—not too sticky or crumbly or granular, just a quintessential rice that is fluffy and ready to soak up the sauces or soups you serve it with. Rice is less a food and more a vessel to pick up other flavors in a dish, and this is the perfect type of rice to do it. Jasmine is just moist enough to fully take on the flavors of whatever dish she meets. And we love her for that.

1. Place the rice in a fine-mesh sieve and run it under water. With your hand, move the rice in a circular motion until the water runs clear. This step does two things: It cleans the rice and washes out some of the starch to achieve a nice fluffy texture (instead of heavy, wet rice).

2. Dump the rice into a small pot and add 2¾ cups [660 ml] of water and the salt. Stir with a spoon to evenly distribute the salt in the rice. Place the uncovered pot on the stove over medium-high heat and bring to a boil. Cover the pot, decrease the heat to low, and let her cook undisturbed for 13 minutes.

3. After 13 minutes, shut the heat off and let the covered pot sit undisturbed for another 10 minutes.

4. Remove the lid and, using a fork, fluff the rice. Voilà! You've got yourself a perfectly cooked and aromatic pot of steamed jasmine rice. Transfer leftovers to an airtight container and refrigerate for up to 4 days.

Crispy Garlic Rice Frittata with Herb Salad

SERVES 4 TO 6

FRITTATA

9 eggs

1 cup [240 ml] heavy cream

½ cup [100 g] grated aged white cheddar

2 tsp kosher salt

2 tsp white pepper

3 Tbsp extra-virgin olive oil

3 garlic cloves, minced

2 cups [240 g] Stovetop Jasmine Rice / RECIPE ON PAGE 75

½ cup [110 g] unsalted butter, cold, cubed

HERB SALAD

1 Fresno chile, thinly sliced crosswise

¼ cup [5 g] Thai basil leaves

¼ cup [5 g] cilantro leaves

¼ cup [5 g] mint leaves

Juice of 1 lime

¼ cup [60 ml] extra-virgin olive oil

Kosher salt

Freshly ground black pepper

Early in my catering days, when I would do breakfasts, I would get really nervous at the idea of making a bunch of scrambles or omelets first thing in the morning. So my solution was to make frittatas, which everyone really loved. They're substantial but not heavy, super versatile, and a great way to start the day (and saved me from playing short-order cook).

For all those brunch girlies out there, this is my Fil-Am version of frittata. (Fil-Am is how we Filipino Americans refer to ourselves.) I love this girl because she's a riff on eggs and rice, something I ate all the time growing up. This requires lots of butter and cream and delivers crunchy cooked rice and fluffy, custardy eggs. It's got fat, protein, and carbs—the holy trinity, a full meal! It's a perfect thing for a boozy brunch or even a hangover brunch. And here's my last little tip: Cook and serve this in a cast-iron skillet; there's something so magical about that presentation.

1. TO MAKE THE FRITTATA: Preheat the oven to 350°F [180°C].

2. In a large bowl, lightly whisk the eggs, heavy cream, and half of the cheddar. Season with 1 tsp of the salt and 1 tsp of the white pepper. Set aside.

3. Add 1 Tbsp of the olive oil to a cast-iron skillet and use a paper towel to rub the olive oil all over the inside of the skillet. Add the remaining 2 Tbsp of oil and warm over medium heat. Add the garlic and fry until crispy golden brown, about 1 minute. Stir frequently to ensure that the garlic does not burn.

4. Add the rice and season with the remaining 1 tsp salt and 1 tsp white pepper. Stir with a spatula to get the rice nicely lubricated with the garlic and oil. Using the spatula, spread the rice so it covers the bottom of the skillet in a layer about ½ in [13 mm] thick. Let the rice cook undisturbed for 3 to 4 minutes until the bottom of the rice gets crispy.

5. Pour the egg mixture over the top and let it cook for 2 to 3 minutes until the edges start to firm up. Sprinkle the remaining cheese on top of the egg mixture. Bake for 15 to 20 minutes until the edges of the eggs are brown and the cheese has melted. Let rest at room temperature for about 10 minutes.

6. MEANWHILE, TO MAKE THE HERB SALAD: In a medium bowl, combine the Fresno chile, basil, cilantro, and mint. Squeeze the lime juice and drizzle the olive oil over the top. Season with salt and pepper to taste and delicately toss the salad with your hands. Set aside.

7. Invert the frittata onto a serving platter so that the crispy rice is visible. Slice into wedges and serve on plates while still warm or at room temperature. Garnish with the herb salad and chow down!

8. Slice leftover frittata into individual portion sizes and store with the remaining herb salad in an airtight container in the refrigerator for up to 3 days.

Garlic Furikake Rice *with Fried Egg*

SERVES 4

3 cups [540 g] Stovetop Jasmine Rice / RECIPE ON PAGE 75

½ cup [25 g] Easy Crispy Garlic / RECIPE ON PAGE 57

1 tsp kosher salt

3 green onions, thinly sliced, for garnish

1 Tbsp ABC Sweet Soy Sauce, for garnish

Furikake, for garnish

4 large eggs, fried sunny-side up, for serving

My parents both worked when I was a kid, and so our weekday breakfasts were usually rushed—a grab-and-go situation. But on weekends, my mom really turned it out. She would make us sinangag, or garlic fried rice, and serve it with fried Spam, a fried egg, and the sausage known as longanisa. It was an elaborate spread and made with so much love. I can remember lying in bed and hearing my mom call our names, and then later, when we inevitably didn't get up, my dad would shout and we would groggily make our way to the breakfast table that was overflowing with food. I remember a lot of eating with our hands and just laughing and talking and catching up about the events of the last week.

This is what I wish for you when you're eating this delightful fried rice—a table filled with joyful connection. This recipe is a great way to use leftover rice, because fried rice is best when made with really dry leftovers. When scorched on a hot pan, it magically becomes crumbly, flaky, granular, crispy, crunchy . . . what a stunning transformation. I love to add a little furikake for added flavor—it's usually made of seaweed and bonito, so it has a fishy, umami flavor that then melds with the pungent garlic. If you think rice is boring, wow, get ready to be astonished at how much flavor and texture is packed into this easy-to-make dish. I know that rice is often thought of as the side dish, but this proves that she has some real star quality when treated right.

1. In a large nonstick saucepan, add the rice and half of the crispy garlic. Season with the salt and gently mix together with a rubber spatula. Cook over medium heat for about 5 minutes.

2. Transfer the garlic rice onto a platter and sprinkle with the reserved crispy garlic and the green onions. Drizzle the sweet soy sauce on top of the rice. Finish it off with a dusting of furikake to your liking. Divide the rice among four bowls and enjoy it right away with a fried egg on top.

Radish and Herb Salad *with Sweet Buttered Nuts*

SERVES 4

1 large shallot

2 Tbsp lemon juice

½ tsp kosher salt, plus more to taste

½ tsp sugar

1 bunch hakurei turnips, trimmed (see Note)

1 small bunch red radishes, trimmed

1 watermelon radish

½ cup [10 g] Italian parsley leaves

½ cup [10 g] cilantro leaves

3 Tbsp extra-virgin olive oil

Freshly ground black pepper

½ cup [125 g] Sweet Buttered Nuts / RECIPE ON PAGE 57

During the colder months, I really amp up the soups and stews in my repertoire. It makes sense: Not only is it colder outside, but Mother Nature also provides us with heartier ingredients this time of year, which are perfect for making stews. That's what cooking with the seasons is all about. But I do think that something really bright, like this salad, helps balance out a filling soup or stew and make it feel like a proper meal. In fact, I recommend serving this easy-to-make salad alongside any hearty fare during the winter. I love the crunch, brightness, sharpness, and acidity it provides—it makes you feel alive! Double the recipe and leave the greens undressed in the fridge. They'll stay fresh for a few days, and you can just dress it right before serving.

NOTE: Hakurei turnips are a variety of small Japanese salad turnips. If you can't find these at your local market or Asian grocer, substitute small white turnips. Delfino cilantro is pictured and preferred, but any cilantro will work.

1. Use a mandoline to thinly slice the shallot. Transfer the shallot to a small bowl. Add the lemon juice, salt, and sugar. Toss to combine, then set aside uncovered at room temperature for 30 minutes.

2. Using the mandoline, carefully cut the turnips, red radishes, and watermelon radish into coins about ⅛ in [4 mm] thick. Transfer them to a medium bowl. Sprinkle in half of the parsley and half of the cilantro and toss to combine. Reserve the rest of the herbs for garnish.

3. Add the pickled shallots to the bowl with the radishes and herbs. Drizzle in the olive oil. Season with salt and black pepper to taste. Give it a good hand mix and transfer to a serving platter. Spoon the sweet buttered nuts over the top of the salad and garnish with the remaining herbs. Serve immediately.

82

Radicchio and Satsuma Salad
with Seedy Coconut Confetti and Ricotta Salata

SERVES 4 TO 6

1 head purple radicchio, torn or cut into ¾ in [2 cm] pieces

2 shallots, thinly sliced

½ cup [120 ml] Pancit Dressing / RECIPE ON PAGE 52

2 satsuma oranges, peeled and segmented

2 oz [55 g] ricotta salata

2 Tbsp Seedy Coconut Confetti / RECIPE ON PAGE 60

OK, so winter needs a powerful salad, not just some lightly dressed leaves. No shade, that's great for summer, but in winter, we need a salad with swagger, with power, with charisma. We need a salad with BDE. So this is it, friends, a salad that's too much but also just enough. It's bitter, it's tart, it's salty, it's sweet, it's crunchy. It's everything I lust for in a well-endowed, robust, filling winter salad. Everything from the royal purple of the radicchio to the sunburst flecks of satsuma oranges beckons you to come closer and dig in. And flavor-wise, this is the opposite of a simple summer salad where we let the ingredients stand on their own. This is about adding in lots of contradictory elements that, somehow, work together. The end result is just a bomb of excitement—it's energetic, zingy, surprising, and, best of all, celebratory and fun! I cannot tell you how much this salad gets my motor going.

In a big bowl, combine the radicchio and shallots. Spoon over half of the dressing and, with your clean hands, give the salad some love with a generous massage. Transfer the salad to a platter. Haphazardly scatter the segmented satsumas over the salad. Drizzle with the remaining dressing. With a vegetable peeler, shave the ricotta salata over the top to give her a nice salty bite, then to finish, shower her with the seedy coconut confetti. Serve immediately.

Laing

Laing is truly one of my favorite dishes in the world. Traditionally made of taro leaves stewed in coconut milk, ginger, and chiles, it's basically the Filipino version of creamed spinach (taro leaves are very similar in flavor and texture to spinach). In some versions, cut-up pieces of shrimp or pork add richness and flavor, and depending on the person making it, it can be quite spicy. Its creaminess and stew-like quality, which warms you from the inside, is a heavenly combination. Pure decadence. That's my main memory of laing from growing up—just how luscious it seemed. Oh, and it is often made in a single pot or pan, which I love.

While the Philippines is a subtropical country, laing is a surprisingly good cold-weather meal. Make it on a chilly winter's night when you're craving something easy and hearty and just a little indulgent. It's a great side dish, but I've also been known to have a bowl of laing and rice as my main meal.

To be totally honest, laing is not much to look at. It's a globby, sloppy pile of cooked greens, but, man, is it a flavor bomb. If you go to a Fil-Am gathering where food is served family or buffet style, you can almost always bet there will be a big mound of laing there. She may not be a beauty queen, but don't skip her! I've included a prettier, lighter version of it in this book, on page 85. Mine is more of a "deconstructed laing" or, really, a saladified laing. Regardless, it contains classic Filipino flavors and interesting textures, and it makes me smile every time I have it.

Warm Kale Laing Salad

SERVES 4

½ cup [70 g] raw unsalted cashews, coarsely chopped

3 Tbsp unrefined coconut oil

1 small shallot, minced

5 garlic cloves, minced

1 Tbsp peeled and minced fresh ginger

2 Thai chiles

One 14 oz [420 ml] can unsweetened coconut milk

2 Tbsp reduced sodium miso paste

½ tsp kosher salt, plus more to taste

½ tsp freshly ground black pepper, plus more to taste

2 lb [910 g] dinosaur kale, stemmed, leaves coarsely chopped

2 limes

This is an adaptation of laing, a dish I love so much. Whereas laing is traditionally more like a creamed green, I've given it a little salad-y makeover. My version takes a more refreshing approach but doesn't skimp on flavor—the velvety coconut broth with ginger, chile, garlic, and miso serves as the dressing to the sturdy dinosaur kale. Dressing the leafy greens in the warm coconut milk does two things: It gives them a luscious coating and delicately softens them, while still leaving that nice hearty bite that a kale salad delivers. This can be eaten on its own as a big salad (with or without a protein) or as a nice side piece to steamy, aromatic jasmine rice as a main meal, if you catch my drift. I know that kale salads are everywhere these days, but this is a really unique approach that will make you instantly forget all the other ones!

1. In a small heavy-bottom pan over medium heat, add the cashews. Stirring frequently, toast the cashews for 3 to 4 minutes until fragrant. Remove from the heat and cool.

2. In a large saucepan over medium heat, add the coconut oil and shallot and sauté for 1 to 2 minutes until translucent. Add the garlic, ginger, and chiles and cook until fragrant, about 3 minutes.

3. Add the coconut milk and miso and whisk together until the mixture emulsifies. Simmer for at least 5 minutes until the sauce is bubbly. Season with the salt and black pepper.

4. Add the kale and coat it completely with the coconut broth. Using a Microplane, zest the limes over the kale and stir. Season the kale with more salt and black pepper to taste. Squeeze the lime juice over the top. Divide among four bowls and garnish with the toasted cashews. This salad is best eaten the day it's made, but you can also store leftovers in an airtight container in the refrigerator for up to 3 days.

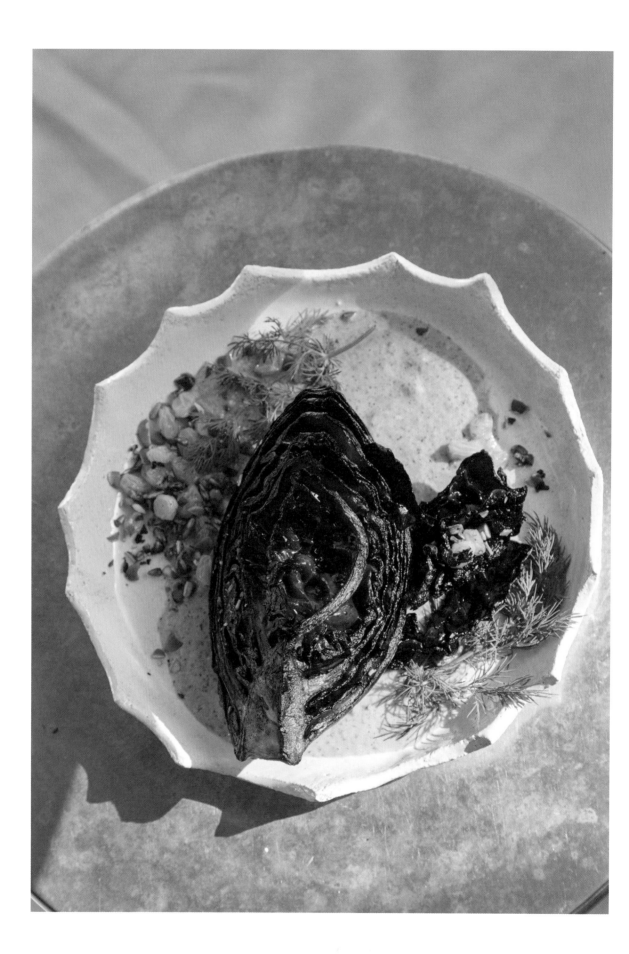

Braised Red Cabbage *with Coconut Green Goddess Dressing*

SERVES 4

1 medium purple cabbage, cut into four wedges

Kosher salt

Freshly ground black pepper

3 Tbsp avocado oil

1 cup [240 ml] apple cider vinegar

1 dried makrut lime leaf

3 Tbsp pumpkin seeds

½ cup [120 ml] Coconut Green Goddess Dressing / RECIPE ON PAGE 44

2 Tbsp Pickled Golden Raisins / RECIPE ON PAGE 62

¼ cup [5 g] dill, roughly chopped

I love the idea of taking something humble, like cabbage, which is usually thought of as a side, and then really doing it up and making her a star! It's like when the nerdy girl in a teen movie takes off her glasses and—surprise!—she's stunning. Here, the way you "take off her glasses" is you sear the hell out of her and give her outer leaves some real charred, caramelized, crispy crunch. Then you roast her so the middle is a little softer, tender, and succulent. Finally, you drizzle a creamy coconut green goddess dressing on top before finishing her off with some sumptuous raisins and crunchy toasted pumpkin seeds—a real party of flavors and textures! The royal purple color of the cabbage is striking. Look at this nerdy girl becoming a star.

1. Preheat the oven to 400°F [205°C]. Turn on your kitchen vent because it's going to be a smoky ride. Season the cabbage generously with salt and pepper and set aside.

2. In a large ovenproof sauté pan or cast-iron skillet over medium-high heat, add the oil. Once the oil is shimmering, lay the cabbage cut side down and sear each side for 3 minutes until slightly charred and crisp all the way around. Carefully pour the apple cider vinegar into the skillet. At this point, the vinegar will pop off, so move your body away from the pan. Throw in the makrut lime leaf. Transfer the skillet to the oven and roast for 25 minutes.

3. Meanwhile, in a small pan over medium-low heat, toast the pumpkin seeds for 3 to 5 minutes, or until you can smell the aroma of toasted pumpkin seeds.

4. Remove the cabbage from the oven and let her rest for 10 minutes. Discard the makrut lime leaf. Transfer the cabbage to a platter and pour any drippings from the skillet over the cabbage, then drizzle with the dressing. Spoon the pickled raisins over. Sprinkle with the dill and toasted pumpkin seeds and chow down! This is best enjoyed right away.

Kamote *with Whipped Tahini*

SERVES 4

4 medium sweet potatoes

3 Tbsp extra-virgin olive oil

1 tsp kosher salt

1 tsp freshly ground black pepper

Whipped Tahini / RECIPE ON PAGE 50

1 lime

1 jalapeño, thinly sliced on a bias

2 green onions, chopped on a bias

½ cup [10 g] cilantro leaves

Flaky sea salt, to taste

In Tagalog, the word *kamote* means "sweet potato." There's this snack in the Philippines of fried sweet potatoes served with brown sugar. This is my little spin on that, but instead of frying the taters, I roast them to bring out their natural sweetness and serve them with my Whipped Tahini so it's almost like a potato dipped in "cheese" sauce. I think that "cheesy" flavor and the sweetness pair beautifully. You know how people alternate between sweet and salty snacks? This is that, but in one dish.

I served this once at the fashion influencer/writer Leandra Medine's house and I am telling you, people just died for it. They were fingers-in-the-bowl, licking-their-plates going wild. I loved seeing it. The key here is to lay the cut side of the potato down to get it nice and caramelized, and I think it's fun to scatter some green onions and herbs on top before serving so it's a vibrant, messy pile of goodness. This dish . . . she's giving "cheese" and potatoes, but bougie!

1. Preheat the oven to 425°F [220°C].

2. With a sharp knife, cut the sweet potatoes in half lengthwise and then cut each half lengthwise at a 45-degree angle so you end up with four long wedges per half. Throw the sweet potatoes onto a baking sheet, lubricate them with the olive oil, and season with the salt and pepper. Toss to coat, then flip the sweet potatoes cut side down and place the baking sheet on the middle rack of the oven. Roast for 25 minutes, or until the bottoms of the sweet potatoes are caramelized and soft.

3. Schmear the whipped tahini onto a large serving platter and place the sweet potatoes on top skin side down. Using a Microplane, zest the lime over the sweet potatoes, then slice the lime in half and squeeze the lime juice right on top. Sprinkle the jalapeño, green onions, and cilantro over the top. Finish her off with a pinch of flaky sea salt for a happy ending and serve! Store leftovers in an airtight container in the refrigerator for up to 2 weeks.

Lola's Vegetable Lumpia

MAKES 25 LUMPIA, SERVES 6 TO 8

Neutral oil, such as canola or grapeseed oil, for frying

1 small yellow onion, diced

5 garlic cloves, minced

One 3 in [7.5 cm] piece fresh ginger, peeled and minced

1 lb [455 g] bean sprouts

One 15 oz [430 g] can chickpeas, drained

1 cup [110 g] shredded orange carrots

1 cup [100 g] chopped Chinese celery

½ cup [50 g] finely chopped green onions

½ cup [6 g] cilantro, finely chopped

Kosher salt

Freshly ground black pepper

Twenty-five 8 in [20 cm] spring roll wrappers

Sweet and Spicy Banana Ketchup / RECIPE ON PAGE 49, for dipping

Vinegar Sauce / RECIPE ON PAGE 52, for dipping

I used to watch my lola roll her lumpia, one by one, into edible "presents." Lumpia, is, in essence, a fried spring roll. The crispy outer layer is like the wrapping paper for the vegetable mixture within. They're a total crowd-pleaser and the perfect appetizer for celebrations with friends and family. Bring them to a party and people will lose their minds.

They're usually made with meat, but I use traditional, humble root vegetables here—carrots, celery—and then add chickpeas for a little hearty protein and a meaty quality, when cooked with my holy trinity: onions, garlic, and ginger. It's the most delightful little pocket of flavor inside crackly, crunchy skin. I'm drooling already.

This pairs well with all those sauces from the Sawsawan section, and, honestly, this would be a really fun, interactive thing to cook with friends. Frying lumpia as you play music and drink wine: What says "holidays" more than that? You can also fold big batches and freeze them. Then just fry up a few when you're in a snacky mood.

Making these for friends carries on my lola's legacy— so much of cooking is about nurturing and caring for people, so I feel like I'm taking that love, comfort, and warmth that she gave me and passing it onto my friends and family. It's taking her love and keeping it alive.

1. In a large pan over medium heat, add 3 Tbsp of neutral oil. Add the onion and sauté until translucent, about 3 minutes. Add the garlic and ginger and cook until fragrant, another minute or two. Add the bean sprouts, chickpeas, carrots, and Chinese celery to the pan and stir. Cook for 5 minutes or until the vegetables are soft but still have a bite to them. Transfer the cooked vegetables to a medium mixing bowl and let cool completely.

2. When the vegetables are completely cool, add the green onions and cilantro to the bowl, then season with salt and pepper to taste.

3. Gently peel apart the spring roll wrappers. Keep the wrappers covered with a damp cloth or in the plastic wrapper, working with one spring roll wrapper at a time.

continued

Winter

4. Place a wrapper on a clean, flat surface in front of you. Place ¼ cup [40 g] of the vegetable filling in the center of the wrapper and spread the filling horizontally to form a log.

5. Fold up the bottom over the filling and roll two times. Fold in the sides. Using a pastry brush or clean fingertips, brush the top edge with water and roll up the wrapper tightly. Transfer the lumpia seam side down onto a parchment paper–lined baking sheet and continue with the remaining wrappers and filling. Make sure they don't touch so they don't stick to each other.

6. At this point, you can freeze the lumpia if you are preparing them in advance. Lay the lumpia in a single layer on the baking sheet. Place the baking sheet uncovered in the freezer for 2 hours until they are firm. Transfer the frozen lumpia to freezer-safe bags. Label the bags with the date and store in the freezer for up to 1 month. To cook frozen lumpia, add 2 to 3 minutes to the frying time.

7. To cook the fresh lumpia, in a heavy-bottom, high-sided pan over medium heat, warm 2 to 3 in [5 to 7.5 cm] of neutral oil for about 7 minutes, or until it reads 350°F [180°C] on a frying thermometer. Working in batches, fry 3 to 5 lumpia at a time, making sure not to overcrowd the pan. Fry each side for about 4 minutes until golden brown, 8 minutes total.

8. Transfer the finished lumpia to a paper towel–lined baking sheet and immediately season with salt. Serve them hot or at room temperature with the two dips. Once fried, these are best enjoyed immediately.

Mushroom Adobo

SERVES 4

6 Tbsp [90 ml] neutral oil, such as canola or grapeseed oil

2 lb [910 g] mixed mushrooms, such as maitake, king oyster, and baby portobellos, torn or thinly sliced

1 tsp kosher salt, plus more to taste

Freshly ground black pepper

1 small yellow onion, chopped

5 garlic cloves, finely minced

½ cup [120 ml] tamari

½ cup [120 ml] distilled white vinegar

3 Tbsp maple syrup

One 14 oz [420 ml] can unsweetened coconut milk

1 tsp chili flakes

1 Tbsp black peppercorns

3 bay leaves

Stovetop Jasmine Rice / RECIPE ON PAGE 75, for serving

2 bunches green onions, chopped on a bias, for garnish

1. In a large sauté pan over medium-high heat, heat 2 Tbsp of the oil until shimmering.

2. Add half the mushrooms to the pan and let sizzle for 3 minutes, untouched. Stir occasionally until they reach the point of caramelization, 6 to 7 minutes total. Season with the salt and freshly ground black pepper and transfer to a plate. Add an additional 2 Tbsp of oil and repeat with the remaining mushrooms. Set aside.

3. Lower the heat to medium and add the remaining 2 Tbsp of oil to the same sauté pan. Add the onion and sweat into a jammy-caramelized goodness, about 3 minutes. Add the garlic, stir, and let them marry with the onions, 3 to 5 minutes.

4. Deglaze the pan by adding the tamari and vinegar, scraping the bottom of the pan with a wooden spoon. Sweeten her up by adding the maple syrup, and thicken her up with the coconut milk. Stir the adobo sauce really well. Add the chili flakes, black peppercorns, and bay leaves. Lower the heat to medium-low and let the sauce reduce for about 15 minutes until it is velvety and the aromatics have penetrated into the sauce.

5. Add the cooked mushrooms to the pool of adobo sauce and let everybody in the pan harmonize and warm up for 3 to 5 minutes. Give her a taste and season her with more salt and pepper to taste.

6. Divide the mushroom adobo among four bowls. Serve with rice and garnish with green onions. Devour to your heart's desire. This is best enjoyed right away.

94

Usually, adobo is made with a meat, but a few years ago, I started using mushrooms instead at private dinners and events, and people really responded to it. Since then, mushrooms have gotten quite popular in the culinary community, which is great, and I'm glad to see people are exploring varieties beyond the usual white button or portobello mushrooms. I'm using mixed mushroom here because of the various textures of meatiness. The umami flavor of the mushrooms pairs really well with the pungent adobo sauce. I love the way the adobo just glides over the mushrooms; it's velvety, silky, welcoming, and enticing.

Miso Coconut Pancit

SERVES 4

Kosher salt

1 lb [455 g] spaghetti

3 Tbsp extra-virgin olive oil

5 garlic cloves, minced

One 2 in [5 cm] piece fresh ginger, peeled and minced

One 14 oz [420 ml] can unsweetened coconut milk

3 Tbsp Miso Mushroom Bagoong / RECIPE ON PAGE 54

Freshly ground white pepper

1 lemon

1 Tbsp pink peppercorns

Pancit is stir-fried vermicelli noodles, a classic Filipino dish and a great, easy meal for a weeknight. Here, I use spaghetti noodles. The star is this creamy, dreamy, umami miso-coconut sauce with its spicy specks of pink peppercorn! (Oh my God, my mouth is literally watering.) It's so thick and delicious, you really want it to coat all the noodles. It's almost like a Filipino-American-ish version of fettuccine alfredo.

This recipe is slightly inspired by a dish my Uncle Junior used to make all the time. At a pop-up a few years ago, I riffed on it and really pumped up the creamy, coconutty aspects, and I think the result packs a lot of punchy, exciting flavor into a relatively simple dish. I like to think of her as an updated version of the pasta dishes with Classico Sauce my mom used to make for me as a kid, but with my own spin on it. Stick a fork in this baby, she's done.

1. Bring a large pot of salted water to a boil. Cook the spaghetti according to the package directions. Reserve ⅓ cup [80 ml] of the noodle water, then drain the noodles.

2. In a large sauté pan over medium heat, warm the olive oil until shimmering. Add the garlic and ginger and fry, stirring with a wooden spoon, until golden brown, about 2 minutes. Whisk in the coconut milk and miso mushroom bagoong. Bring the sauce to a simmer and cook until she reaches a thick and creamy consistency, about 3 minutes.

3. Toss in the spaghetti and mix until each strand of pasta is coated with the sauce. If the sauce is too thick, splash in a couple of tablespoons of the reserved pasta water. Season with salt and white pepper to taste.

4. Using a Microplane, zest the lemon over the spaghetti, then cut the lemon in half, discard any seeds, and squeeze the lemon juice over the top. Sprinkle in the pink peppercorns and stir to combine. Divide the spaghetti among four bowls and enjoy! This is best enjoyed right away.

Lugaw *with Seedy Chili Oil*

SERVES 6

2 Tbsp extra-virgin olive oil

One 5 in [12 cm] piece fresh ginger, peeled and finely minced (about 3 Tbsp)

6 garlic cloves, finely minced

1 cup [200 g] uncooked jasmine rice

¼ cup [50 g] uncooked sushi rice

2 Tbsp kosher salt

OPTIONAL TOPPINGS

Green onions, sliced on a bias

Seedy Chili Oil / RECIPE ON PAGE 56

ABC Sweet Soy Sauce

Pickled Golden Raisins / RECIPE ON PAGE 62

Porridges and soups are the ultimate winter dishes for two reasons. First, they're so easy to make and really hard to mess up. And second, they keep you warm and provide a feeling of comfort during the colder months. Savory rice porridge is a popular Filipino dish—we call it lugaw—but you'll find a version in many other Asian countries (think of congee, a staple of Chinese cuisine, for instance).

I like lugaw for its simplicity and the fact that it's like a blank canvas and topping it is where you can get creative! I love topping mine with seedy chili oil and green onions, or sprinkling pickled golden raisins over the top for tartness and chew. A lugaw can really do anything, she's so versatile. Flip back to the Sawsawan chapter on pages 42–69, and literally every one of those recipes would be a great way to add a little punch. Chop up a bunch of herbs and mix them in. Or host a lugaw party where you have a big pot of it bubbling away and a bunch of different toppings for guests to DIY their own bowls. Are lugaw parties a thing? Sure, let's make them a thing!

1. In a large Dutch oven over medium heat, warm the olive oil. Add the ginger, garlic, jasmine rice, and sushi rice. This method of cooking will do two things: 1. cook the ginger and garlic, and 2. toast the rice. Using a rubber spatula, stir and cook for 2 to 3 minutes. The aroma of ginger and garlic will start to blossom. Sprinkle in 1 Tbsp of the salt and stir the mixture again. Pour in 10 cups [2.4 L] of water and sprinkle in the remaining 1 Tbsp salt. Stir her well, then decrease the heat to medium-low, bring to a simmer, and cook for about 80 minutes.

2. Stir occasionally to make sure the rice doesn't stick to the bottom of the pot. You want the lugaw to be the consistency of cooked oatmeal—thick and gloopy.

3. Divide the lugaw among six small bowls and garnish with the toppings of your choice. Serve immediately! This is best enjoyed right away.

Winter

Sotanghon Soup

SERVES 4

2 Tbsp avocado oil

One 3 in [7.5 cm] piece fresh ginger, peeled and minced

1 head garlic, cloves peeled and finely minced

1 small shallot, chopped

6 cups [1.4 L] low-sodium vegetable stock

4 oz [115 g] mung bean noodles (HNSTY Longkow Vermicelli)

Hot water

Kosher salt

Freshly ground black pepper

1 Tbsp fish sauce

Seedy Chili Oil / RECIPE ON PAGE 56, for serving

3 green onions, thinly sliced, for serving

Seedy Coconut Confetti / RECIPE ON PAGE 60, for serving

1 lemon, cut into wedges, for serving

This is my version of chicken noodle soup, with glass noodles cooked in vegetable broth. My mom used to make homemade chicken broth, dumping the whole chicken—the works—in boiling water, and then squeezing tons of calamansi on top to add some bright zing. And I swear to God, that broth cleared up anything. I like to think mine does too—a head cold, a sniffle, even one of those mornings where you just feel a bit off. My favorite part about this dish has got to be the noodles and how they slip and slide in your mouth. And then that touch of squeezed lemon juice and a crunchy seedy coconut confetti on top of the soup? Heaven. It brings me right back to my mom's kitchen when I was a kid.

1. In a large Dutch oven over medium heat, warm the avocado oil, about 1 minute. Add the ginger, garlic, and shallot. Sauté for 3 to 5 minutes until fragrant. Pour in the vegetable stock and stir. Bring to a low simmer, cover, and simmer for 20 minutes for the flavors to come together.

2. Meanwhile, in a large bowl, add the noodles and pour in enough hot water to cover. Let the noodles sit for 3 to 5 minutes, then drain and set aside.

3. After the stock has simmered for 20 minutes, add the noodles to the broth and stir. Season with salt, pepper, and the fish sauce.

4. Divide the soup among four bowls. Drizzle with the seedy chili oil and sprinkle the green onions and seedy coconut confetti over the top. Add a squeeze of lemon juice to each bowl and serve! This is best enjoyed right away.

Mung Bean and Vegetable Soup

SERVES 4 TO 6

3 Tbsp avocado oil

1 small yellow onion, chopped

3 garlic cloves, minced

One 2 in [5 cm] piece fresh ginger, peeled and minced

1 Tbsp chili flakes

1 bay leaf or ⅛ tsp bay leaf powder

2 medium sweet potatoes, cut into ½ in [13 mm] cubes

2 medium carrots, scrubbed and roughly chopped

2 medium celery stalks, roughly chopped

1 cup [200 g] dried mung beans (see Note)

5 cups [1.2 L] low-sodium vegetable stock

One 14 oz [420 ml] can unsweetened coconut milk

3 Tbsp Miso Mushroom Bagoong / RECIPE ON PAGE 54

½ tsp kosher salt, plus more to taste

½ tsp freshly ground black pepper, plus more to taste

Crusty sourdough bread or Stovetop Jasmine Rice / RECIPE ON PAGE 75, for serving

½ cup [10 g] cilantro, roughly chopped, for garnish

My lola used to make this soup for us every Friday, no matter what—in Tagalog, we call it *ginisang munggo*. Let's just say I had a complicated relationship with it—I loved it because it was comforting and became a ritual, an expected thing, but I hated it because it was just this thing that was always there, even when I didn't want it. Whenever I got home from school on Friday, I knew it'd be waiting, and I'd have it like a second lunch before my parents picked me up.

Over the years, I've learned to appreciate the beauty of having something warming and soothing on a regular basis. This soft bean soup, with lots of ginger and pepper, is a comforting dish, my food equivalent to a chunky, oversized turtleneck. She's a real watch-a-rom-com-while-it-snows sort of soup. I've amped up the vegetables here with sweet potatoes, carrots, and celery, so it's hearty and filling, and then added coconut milk for a luscious, velvety texture. It's sort of in the split-pea-soup family. It's a great thing to have on the stove when you have guests over; it fills the room with its aroma while you have drinks and snacks, and you don't have to fuss with it much. Serve it with jasmine rice or crusty sourdough bread.

NOTE: You can find mung beans at most Asian markets or even online, but if you need to, you can swap in chickpeas or any Rancho Gordo bean.

continued

1. In a Dutch oven over medium heat, warm the avocado oil. Add the onion and let it sweat and caramelize for 5 to 7 minutes. Stir frequently.

2. Add the garlic, ginger, chili flakes, and bay leaf. Cook and stir for 2 minutes until aromatic. Throw in the sweet potatoes, carrots, and celery. Sauté until the vegetables are cooked through and can be pierced easily with a fork, about 5 minutes.

3. Sprinkle in the mung beans and stir for about 1 minute. Pour in the vegetable stock and coconut milk and whisk in the miso mushroom bagoong until it melts into the broth. Season with the salt and pepper. Bring to a boil, then decrease the heat to low and cover. Cook for about 1 hour at a gentle simmer until the mung beans are fully cooked.

4. Add ½ to 1 cup [120 to 240 ml] of water to give it a soupier consistency. Turn the heat off and season with salt and pepper to taste.

5. Divide the soup among four to six bowls. Tear up some sourdough bread or plop a scoop of rice into each bowl and garnish with fresh chopped cilantro.

6. To store, let the soup cool to room temperature and transfer to an airtight container. Store in the refrigerator for up to 3 days.

Bibingka
A Sexy Cake for Sexy People

Can a cake be sexy? Hello, of course it can! I think the sexiest cake of all is moist, spongy, sensual bibingka (followed by juicy, wet tres leches, naturally). For those unfamiliar, bibingka is a very traditional Filipino cake that's made with just a few simple ingredients—mostly rice flour, sugar, eggs, and coconut milk—and it can be spun off in a variety of directions. Glutinous rice flour gives bibingka its happy, squishy mouthfeel and bouncy, chewy texture, which all feels a bit naughty. I always say the perfect density should be almost firm but with a little bit of wobble. You should want to spank it!

Not only does it bring people together, but a bibingka can also be a reflection of so many things, because it's so versatile—it can be vegan (like my recipe on page 162) and it's naturally gluten-free; you can add chocolate or fresh fruit; or you can make it as a pancake or waffle (a little morning-after treat, wink-wink). Each variation has a unique personality and vibe (like a drag queen), so honor its uniqueness! Bibingka is the Madonna of cakes, always changing and evolving. It's great for a birthday, a job promotion, or a wedding or baby shower. Baking is an involved process that requires time, focus, and, crucially, exact measurements; what says you care about someone more than setting aside time and baking for them during these absurd times?

By now you've probably noticed that food gets me in my feels, and bibingka is no different. Yes, it's a joyous and optimistic dish, but it's also a very traditional one that makes me think about my heritage, my history, my family; about who I am and where I come from. As I've baked it over the years and figured out new ways to update and modernize it, I can't help but see it as a reflection of myself and all the messy and beautiful contradictions I contain. My approach changes depending on how I feel when I'm baking it or who I'm baking it for— sometimes I want it to be a little queer, to be silly, to be healthy(ish!), or decadent, or even just a traditional old bibingka like my family used to make, because sometimes the classics are just what you need. You can even make a savory version, which is the original—a bibingka with grated cheddar cheese and a duck egg served at Christmas. For most Filipinos, there's a lot of cultural significance baked in (pun intended!) this dish, but as a first-generation Filipino American, I also see it as a foundation on which I can build new traditions and ideas (like my Bibingka Apple Bread with Maple Glaze on page 265, for example—traditional American flavors in a delicious bibingka loaf). It's thrilling, and it's also tasty.

So here's to bibingka, the sexy, sensual goddess of cakes! Eat her, consume her, revel in all her texture and flavors.

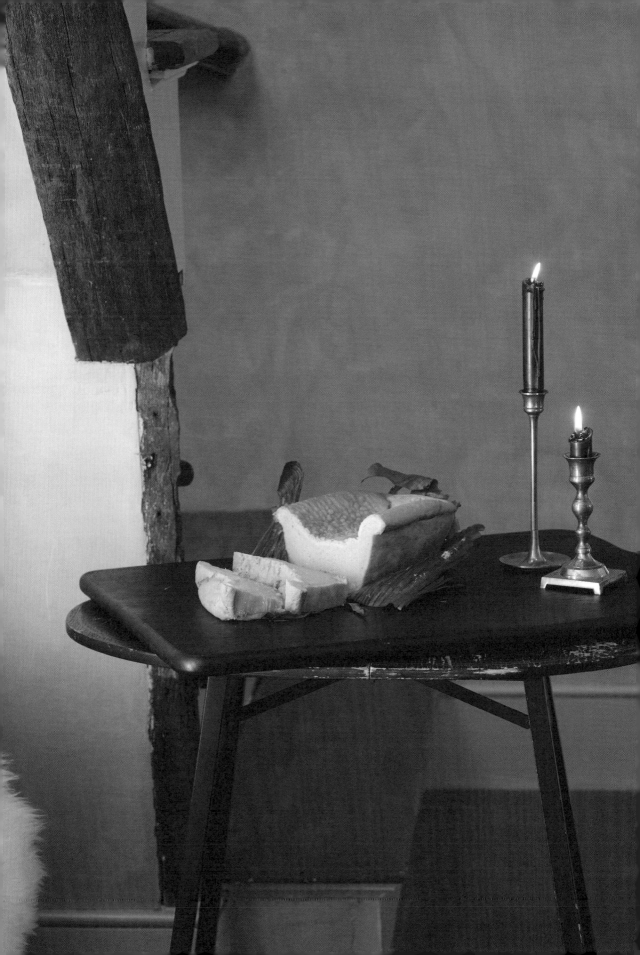

Bibingka Bread

MAKES ONE 8½ BY 4½ IN [21.5 BY 11 CM] LOAF

One 14 by 12 in [35.5 by 30.5 cm] banana leaf

2½ cups [330 g] glutinous rice flour

1 cup [200 g] sugar

1 Tbsp baking powder

1 tsp kosher salt

One 14 oz [420 ml] can unsweetened coconut milk

½ cup [110 g] unsalted butter, melted

3 eggs, at room temperature

1 tsp vanilla extract

Baking bibingka bread was one of the things that got me through the pandemic (sorry, sourdough!). It was a ritual that kept me moving forward, grounded, and focused when the world felt so chaotic. And it became a means of building community when I started selling loaves of it at Cafe Integral, a delightful coffee shop in Nolita, a neighborhood in downtown Manhattan.

The bread is a showstopper: It's baked in a cocoon of banana leaves, which you dramatically peel away to reveal the steaming loaf within. The leaves also give off a tropical floral aroma while baking, which will fill your kitchen—divine! The texture of the bibingka is chewy and bouncy, and I guarantee this is a recipe you'll come back to time and time again! Move over, banana bread, bibingka bread has arrived!

1. If the banana leaf is frozen, bring it to room temperature. Preheat the oven to 350°F [180°C] and position the rack in the middle of the oven. Spray a standard 8½ by 4½ in [21.5 by 11 cm] loaf pan with nonstick coconut oil cooking spray.

2. Using scissors, cut a 12 by 4 in [30.5 by 10 cm] strip from the banana leaf, cutting parallel to the leaf's center vein. Cut the remaining portion of banana leaf into three 12 by 3 in [30.5 by 7.5 cm] strips, again cutting parallel to the leaf's center vein. Wipe down each side of the leaves with a damp paper towel.

3. Place the 3 in [7.5 cm] wide strips crosswise over the bottom and sides of the loaf pan, overlapping as needed to completely line the bottom of the pan. Make sure the leaf ends extend over the sides by 1 to 2 in [2.5 to 5 cm]. Place the remaining banana leaf strip lengthwise along the bottom of the loaf pan and partway up the shorter sides. Set the pan aside.

4. In a large bowl, whisk together the glutinous rice flour, sugar, baking powder, and salt.

5. In a medium bowl, whisk together the coconut milk, melted butter, eggs, and vanilla. Whisk the wet ingredients into the dry ingredients until the mixture is fully incorporated and the batter is smooth.

6. Pour the batter into the prepared loaf pan with the ends of the banana leaves hanging over the edges of the pan. Bake for 1 hour, or until the top and edges are shiny and golden and a wooden skewer inserted into the center comes out clean.

7. Let the bibingka cool completely in the pan. After it is cool, hold the banana leaves and lift the bibingka from the pan. Slice and serve! Leftover bibingka bread will keep tightly wrapped at room temperature for up to 3 days.

Lime Olive Oil Bibingka

MAKES ONE 9 IN [23 CM] ROUND CAKE

BIBINGKA CAKE

1¼ cups [170 g] rice flour

1¼ cups [165 g] glutinous rice flour

1 Tbsp baking powder

1 tsp kosher salt

1 cup [200 g] granulated sugar

3 medium eggs, at room temperature

One 14 oz [420 ml] can unsweetened
  coconut milk

¾ cup [180 ml] extra-virgin olive oil

1 tsp vanilla extract

2 Tbsp lime zest (from about 4 limes)

LIME GLAZE

1 cup [120 g] confectioners' sugar

1 tsp kosher salt (Diamond Crystal)

Zest and juice of 4 limes

Sometimes fate is the best inspiration. Like the time that I ran out of coconut oil while I was baking so I figured, why not sub in some olive oil? I see olive oil cake everywhere anyway, so it was my opportunity to do my version of it. And I thought that lime would be the perfect thing to pair it with, to help cut through that sort of unctuous richness that the oil provides. It's a beautiful, elegant balance. Plus, I love a gorgeous neon-green lime. Sure, she's a bit smaller and doesn't have as much juice as a lemon, but I'm a lime-lover through and through. I love the acidity; it cuts through and gives so much more flavor, something summery and tart and a little vacation-y. And for those thinking, why not lemon? Well, my rebellious side always has me rooting for the underdog.

1. **TO MAKE THE BIBINGKA CAKE:** Preheat the oven to 350°F [180°C] and position the rack in the middle of the oven.

2. Spray a 9 by 2 in [23 by 5 cm] round cake pan with a nonstick olive oil cooking spray. Line the bottom of the cake pan with parchment paper and spray with the cooking spray.

3. In a large bowl, whisk together the rice flour, glutinous rice flour, baking powder, and salt.

4. In a medium bowl, whisk together the granulated sugar and eggs. Add the coconut milk, olive oil, and vanilla. Whisk the wet ingredients into the dry ingredients until the mixture is fully incorporated and the batter is smooth. Fold in the lime zest.

5. Pour the batter into the prepared cake pan and bake for 1 hour to 1 hour and 15 minutes, or until the top and edges are shiny and golden and a wooden skewer inserted into the center comes out clean. Let the bibingka cool completely. After the cake is cool, run a butter knife around the cake to loosen it from the sides of the pan. Gently invert the cake onto a serving plate or cake stand.

6. **TO MAKE THE LIME GLAZE:** Meanwhile, in a small bowl, add the confectioners' sugar, salt, lime zest, and lime juice. Whisk together until combined. Stream in 1 tsp of water and whisk until the glaze is slightly thin in consistency.

7. Smother the completely cooled bibingka with the glaze. Let the glaze drip over the sides. Slice and enjoy! Store the cake in an airtight container at room temperature for up to 3 days.

Macapuno Bibingka

MAKES ONE 9 IN [23 CM] ROUND CAKE

1¼ cups [170 g] rice flour

1¼ cups [165 g] glutinous rice flour

1 cup [200 g] granulated sugar

1 Tbsp baking powder

1 tsp kosher salt

½ cup [110 g] unrefined coconut oil, melted

½ cup [120 ml] seltzer water

1 tsp vanilla extract

One 14 oz [420 ml] can unsweetened coconut milk

One 12 oz [340 g] jar macapuno strings

Coconut Yogurt Cream / RECIPE ON PAGE 69, for garnish

Confectioners' sugar, for garnish

1. Preheat the oven to 350°F [180°C] and position the rack in the middle of the oven. Spray a 9 by 2 in [23 by 5 cm] round cake pan with nonstick spray.

2. In a large bowl, whisk together the rice flour, glutinous rice flour, granulated sugar, baking powder, and salt.

3. In a medium bowl, whisk together the melted coconut oil, seltzer water, vanilla, coconut milk, and macapuno strings. Whisk the wet ingredients into the dry ingredients until the mixture is fully incorporated and the batter is smooth.

4. Pour the batter into the prepared cake pan and bake for 1 hour, or until the top and edges are shiny and golden and a wooden skewer inserted into the center comes out clean.

5. Let the bibingka cool completely in the pan. After the cake is cool, run a butter knife around the cake to loosen it from the sides of the pan. Gently invert the cake onto a serving plate or cake stand. Serve slices with a dollop of coconut yogurt cream and a dusting of confectioners' sugar. Wrap the cake tightly in plastic wrap or store in an airtight container at room temperature for up to 3 days.

Macapuno is a naturally occurring phenomenon where a coconut's flesh turns into a jelly-like, stringy texture with extra sweetness. Don't ask me the specifics—too science-y—but the result is divine. In the Philippines, they jar up macapuno and use it to cook sweet dishes. I have memories of my mom using it a lot in her baking. The texture is kinda slippery, sensual, and a little freaky. By adding it to the batter of a bibingka, it gives the cake an added level of moisture and an unexpectedly delightful, toothsome chew. It's just another way to add to the textural journey of an already scrumptious treat.

Winter

Chocolate Coconut Mousse

SERVES 4 TO 6

One 8 oz [230 g] bag semisweet chocolate chips, preferably Guittard

2 cups [455 g] vanilla coconut yogurt, at room temperature, plus more for garnish

¼ cup [20 g] unsweetened cocoa powder

3 Tbsp coconut jam

1 tsp kosher salt

Dark chocolate shavings, for garnish

Flaky sea salt, for garnish

I'm not sure why, but a chocolate mousse feels very wintry to me—maybe it has something to do with Valentine's Day being in the winter. Or chocolate being a very wintry indulgence . . . but anyway, chocolate is often on my mind this time of year. This is my ode to it.

Here, we layer in two types of coconut flavor, from the yogurt and the jam, to amp up the island-y flavors, and then two types of chocolate, in the form of melted chips and cocoa powder. Shaving a few bits of chocolate over the top adds glamour.

I love that this is indulgent but also fluffy, airy, and cloudlike. It's not a hunk of chocolate cake (which is, of course, perfect for some occasions), but rather, unexpectedly light and lovely. It's good for Valentine's Day as you don't feel too weighed down after the meal. I like to call this my sweet happy ending. ☺ Enjoy!

1. Put the chocolate chips in a heatproof bowl over a double boiler filled with simmering water. Stir the chocolate until glossy and melted. Remove the luscious melted chocolate from the heat and set aside to cool.

2. To a medium mixing bowl, add the yogurt. Using a rubber spatula, pour and scrape the melted chocolate into the yogurt and gently fold the chocolate in until combined.

3. Using a small fine-mesh sieve, sift the cocoa powder into the chocolate-yogurt mixture. Fold the coconut jam and kosher salt into the mixture until fully combined and the

color transforms into a rich chocolate brown. Divide the chocolate yogurt mixture among four to six serving dishes, cover with plastic wrap, and refrigerate overnight. They will keep for up to 2 days.

4. To serve, plop a dollop of vanilla coconut yogurt on top of each chocolate coconut mousse and sprinkle the shaved dark chocolate and flaky sea salt over the top. Serve immediately.

Champorado *with Candied Kumquats*

SERVES 4

One 14 oz [420 ml] can unsweetened coconut milk

1 in [2.5 cm] piece ginger, peeled

½ cup [90 g] 60% bittersweet chocolate chips, preferably Guittard

1 tsp Chinese five-spice powder

1 tsp kosher salt

2 cups [240 g] Stovetop Jasmine Rice / RECIPE ON PAGE 75

1 tsp vanilla extract

Candied Kumquats / RECIPE ON PAGE 68, for serving

Cacao nibs, for serving

Like lugaw, champorado is a rice porridge. Traditionally a breakfast item, this is a sweet version made with chocolate, so I serve it as a dessert. My Lola used to make this for me when it was cold outside, almost like a hot chocolate.

My grandma would usually take leftover rice (because no Filipino household is complete without a big pot of one- or two-day-old rice in the fridge), add some coconut milk and chocolate, and let those ingredients come together on the stove. Spices come next, like hearty, warming ginger and Chinese five-spice powder—it's all about adding layers of flavor to create a really nuanced dining experience. Because I always have to add my little spin, I like to put kumquat in there because, in my mind, chocolate and citrus go together well. It adds a jolt of tartness that cuts through the other flavors and really elevates this dish. It makes me think of being all cozy on a couch reading a book on a cold day, but it also just reminds me of my grandma.

1. In a medium saucepan over medium heat, add the coconut milk and, using a Microplane, grate in the ginger. Bring to a low simmer.

2. Add the chocolate chips, Chinese five-spice powder, and salt, whisking until the chocolate has completely melted. Fold the cooked rice into the mixture with a rubber spatula. Stir frequently until the rice pudding is thick, 5 to 7 minutes. Remove from the heat and stir in the vanilla. Spoon the rice pudding into four bowls and top each with about 1 Tbsp (more is better) of candied kumquats. Sprinkle cacao nibs right on top. Serve warm, or cover and chill in the refrigerator before serving. Champorado is best the day it is made.

Coconut Hot Cocoa

SERVES 2

¼ cup [60 ml] coconut water

2 Tbsp unsweetened cocoa powder

One 14 oz [420 ml] can unsweetened coconut milk

½ cup [90 g] 60% bittersweet chocolate chips, preferably Guittard

1½ tsp kosher salt

Sweetened condensed milk, for serving

When winter chills set in, I daydream of basking on a tropical island. If a warm-weather escape isn't feasible, I turn to my comforting remedy: Coconut Hot Cocoa. This drink combines the richness of hot cocoa with coconut water and coconut milk, instantly transporting me to island bliss. A finishing touch of sweetened condensed milk adds a decadent touch. Perfect for cozy nights wrapped in a blanket indulging in TV time, it's my go-to for warding off the cold and satisfying my island cravings.

1. In a small bowl, whisk together the coconut water and cocoa powder.

2. In a small saucepan over medium heat, whisk together the coconut milk and chocolate chips until the chocolate is completely melted and the mixture is hot, 3 to 5 minutes.

3. Pour the cocoa powder mixture and salt into the hot chocolate. Whisk until smooth. Divide the hot cocoa between two mugs. With a teaspoon, drizzle sweetened condensed milk into each mug to taste. Sip up and be cozy!

Fizzy Calamansi

SERVES 1

2 Tbsp Calamansi Syrup / RECIPE ON PAGE 67

2 Tbsp rice vinegar

¾ oz Aplós Calme (optional)

Sparkling water

Thai basil leaf, for garnish

This recipes takes the zesty, bright ray of sunshine that is the calamansi fruit and turns it into a fun and fizzy nonalcoholic beverage. I think the vinegar and calamansi syrup play off each other beautifully—a little tart and tang! I use a hemp-infused mixer, for all you Dry January-ers, so you still get a calming, even euphoric effect from it, but you can skip it if you prefer (just add more sparkling water instead). You can also add a little tequila or mezcal if you want, and, voilà, it's a calamansi margarita!

In a cocktail shaker, add ice, the calamansi syrup, rice vinegar, and Aplós Calme, if using. Shake and dance her very well for 10 to 20 seconds until well chilled. Fill a glass with ice and strain the calamansi mixture into the glass. Top off with sparkling water and garnish with basil. Sip and enjoy!

Spring

A Time of Renewal, a Time to Watch Things Grow

During the pandemic, when the world became so uncertain and scary overnight, I was blessed with a little escape from New York. A dear friend who had a place upstate invited me to stay with her for a bit until things calmed down (it's easy to forget how weird those days were). She had a small guesthouse and let me spend some time there, which I'm so grateful for. The best part was that she had a garden. Throughout that strange, surreal spring, I watched her plot of land turn lush and green, and then magically bear fruits and vegetables. It was a really healing, awe-inspiring thing to witness. To be with food as it grows and to see the magical abundance that the earth yields is a thing of wonder. If you're given the chance to slow down and watch Mother Nature in action, take it. I dare you not to be absolutely gobsmacked at what she provides us.

The experience reminded me a lot of my lola, who also had a garden, which was a fixture of my childhood. I remember her always tending her garden, being so loving toward it. So often her meals were peppered with things she grew—spring peas, bitter melons, eggplants. Now, as an adult, I've started to understand the intoxicating magic of a garden—the trust that if you plant things, they will grow, and the promise that after a long, dark period, new life will flourish again. Also, in our sped-up world, gardens ask you for patience and allow you to take a beat; they encourage contemplation.

Needless to say, that pandemic spring sparked in me a new, deeper appreciation for vegetables, fruits, freshness, and the bounty of the natural world, as well as a reverence for my newfound life. I really believe that garden saved me during that season of drastic change. I mean, I always loved fresh produce, but I think it really seeped into my bones during that time. It inspired me to not just incorporate these ingredients into my cooking, but to make them the focal point—they are the headlining act, not the backup singers!

This also helped me grapple with some habits I developed as a kid. When I was growing up, I was

overweight. We were a typical Filipino American family in the 1990s—there was lots of fast food, processed food, junk food, and sodas. It was very normal back then. It's taken me a long time to reshape the way I think about eating and food, to transform it into an act that makes me feel nourished and stronger and more comfortable in my own body. I want to really emphasize this: This is not a diet book! But it is full of wholesome recipes that will make you feel good. Being upstate near a garden and farms helped me reconsider my relationship with food. I realized I just liked how I felt when I ate fresher things—energized, stronger, and more connected to my physical self. Writing this book helped me think about how I can continue this habit and how I can share it with others too.

The garden and my time upstate also made me think about the broader implications of our food choices. For example, buying from a local farmer is using my money to support an independent small business as opposed to a big corporation—better still if it's a woman-, POC-, or queer-owned business. Shifting my diet to emphasize fresh produce is better for the environment. Fresh foods make me feel good in my own body, yes, but they also make me feel better about how I'm spending my money and who and what causes I'm supporting. Upstate, it's not uncommon to frequent the same farm stand and get to know the people who grow your food. There's something so beautiful about that. It feeds my soul.

Does that mean I never have sweets? Oh, baby, no. In fact, you'll find some really yummy, decadent sweet treats in this chapter (and throughout this book), many that start with the natural sugar of fruit. Mother Nature has a sweet tooth too! It just means that during spring, as the world around you blooms and, incredibly, comes back to life after a season of hibernation, you should take advantage of its leafy, flourishing bounty. Mother Nature wants you to, and who are we to deny her?

Black Pepper Granola

MAKES 8 CUPS [800 G]

3 cups [300 g] rolled oats

1 cup [60 g] unsweetened coconut flakes

½ cup [70 g] raw unsalted cashews, roughly chopped

½ cup [70 g] pumpkin seeds

½ cup [110 g] unrefined coconut oil

½ cup [120 ml] maple syrup

¼ cup [50 g] packed dark brown sugar

1 Tbsp vanilla extract

3 Tbsp freshly ground black pepper

1 Tbsp kosher salt

1½ cups [170 g] unsweetened banana chips

1 cup [140 g] golden raisins

I love, love, love a crunchy snack you can eat with your hands. Maybe this sounds weird, but to me, it's so fun to have a tub of granola in the car to munch on as you're driving—it helps keep me awake when I'm going longer distances (and I don't even mind that it makes a mess). This granola sort of represents everything I love about a crunchy snack, with peppery, tropical notes and layers of crunch from the various seeds and nuts. The black pepper just brings a spicy savoriness to this sweet granola and I think makes it unique—so don't skip it!

I know some people think granola is just about throwing a bunch of random quantities of different ingredients into a bowl, but I spent a lot of time making sure this recipe was harmonized to perfection! Don't let me down; follow the instructions and you will be rewarded with a fine-tuned crunchy delight! Put this over yogurt for a snack or even eat it with some almond milk like it's cereal—it'll make you feel like a kid again.

1. Preheat the oven to 300°F [150°C] and position the rack in the middle of the oven. Line a baking sheet with parchment paper.

2. In a large bowl, toss together the oats, coconut flakes, cashews, and pumpkin seeds. Set aside.

3. In a small saucepan over low heat, melt the coconut oil. Stir in the maple syrup, brown sugar, and vanilla until the sugar melts completely, about 5 minutes. Remove from the heat and slowly stream the liquid into the bowl with the oat mixture. Mix together with a spatula until the granola is well lubricated and glossy! Stir in the black pepper and salt.

4. Spread this edible confetti mixture evenly onto the prepared baking sheet and bake for 30 to 40 minutes. Halfway through baking, rotate the pan and stir with a spatula. You will know the granola is done when the kitchen is perfumed with sweetness and the granola has caramelized to a honey color.

5. Remove from the oven and let the granola cool completely.

6. Sprinkle the banana chips and raisins over the granola and stir. Store in an airtight container at room temperature for up to 1 month and enjoy!

Spring

Coconut Yogurt *with Rose Goldenberries*

SERVES 4

2 cups [480 g] coconut yogurt

1 Tbsp rose water

Rose Goldenberries / RECIPE ON PAGE 61

1 Tbsp pistachios, toasted and chopped

2 tsp edible dried rose petals, crushed

Creamy, cloudy, and orgasmic is the best way to describe how I like to start my morning! Of course, I'm talking about this Coconut Yogurt with Rose Goldenberries, which is exactly that. This recipe is kinda-sorta based on the traditional Middle Eastern dessert malabi, a rose water milk pudding. The pudding here is the coconut yogurt, and I stir in rose water, which gives the yogurt that floral essence. The goldenberries, aroused and plump after soaking in a rose water syrup, are delectable, chewy morsels. Make the Rose Goldenberries ahead of time—they need to soak for at least 24 hours for maximum flavor. Flecks of chopped pistachios on top give this dish a naughty texture. This recipe leaves you wanting more!

1. In a small bowl, whisk together the coconut yogurt and rose water. Set it aside.

2. Pour 2 Tbsp of the rose goldenberry syrup into four bowls to create pools. Gently spoon the yogurt into the syrup. Sprinkle the goldenberries, pistachios, and rose petals on top and enjoy the orgasmic decadence.

Bibingka Pancakes *with Coconut Palm Sugar Syrup*

SERVES 4

1 cup [135 g] rice flour

1 cup [120 g] glutinous rice flour

½ cup [100 g] sugar

1 Tbsp baking powder

1 tsp kosher salt

One 14 oz [420 ml] can unsweetened coconut milk

½ cup [120 ml] seltzer water

1 tsp vanilla extract

¼ cup [55 g] unrefined coconut oil, for cooking

Coconut Palm Sugar Syrup / RECIPE ON PAGE 68, for serving

Fresh seasonal fruit, such as strawberries, for serving

My most vivid memory of breakfast while growing up is getting pancakes at McDonald's with my twin brother and my grandma. I'd be so excited for those Styrofoam containers and the little syrup packets with tops you peel back. Very highbrow, I know. Though it's not a fancy meal, it still reminds me of being a kid and that feeling of childlike joy. I hope to evoke some of that here, by slightly modifying the classic bibingka recipe and turning it into a pancake. This thin, wet batter yields what I think is the perfect thin pancake, similar to a crepe, with a mochi-like chew and just a bit of a crispy crunch on the outside. The Coconut Palm Sugar Syrup adds a slightly tropical feel to it too—perfect for impressing a date on that first morning after!

1. In a large bowl, whisk together the rice flour, glutinous rice flour, sugar, baking powder, and salt. Pour in the coconut milk, seltzer water, and vanilla and whisk to combine.

2. Heat a skillet over medium heat and add 1 Tbsp of the coconut oil. Add ⅓ cup [80 ml] of batter to the skillet. Cook the pancake until the surface has bubbles and the edges are golden and crispy, 2 to 3 minutes. Flip gently and cook for another 2 minutes. Transfer the pancake to a plate and repeat with the remaining coconut oil and batter.

3. Serve warm with a drizzle of coconut palm sugar syrup and fresh fruit over the top. These are best enjoyed straight off the griddle.

Purple Daikon, Coconut Labneh, and Peanut Salsa Toast

SERVES 4

1 cup [240 g] Coconut Labneh / RECIPE ON PAGE 44

4 thick slices sourdough bread, toasted in a pan with olive oil

2 purple daikon radishes, cut into thin slices with a mandoline or sharp knife

Peanut Salsa / RECIPE ON PAGE 50

1 cup [20 g] cilantro leaves

Flaky sea salt

Freshly ground black pepper

Toast has gotten very trendy these days. It all started with the Australian cafe treat avocado toast, and now there's all sorts of toasts: ricotta toast, sardine toast—I hear the kids on TikTok are even making cottage cheese toast a thing. This is just me giving toast a little Filipino-ish spin, using a rich, creamy coconut labneh atop a crusty hunk of sourdough, adapted from a recipe I created for *Food & Wine* magazine. It's all about layering on a bunch of contrasting elements: sweetness and crunch from the peanut salsa, tartness from the lime, heat from the jalapeño, freshness from the purple daikon. While it's a lot of components, they all come together in a harmonious yet unexpected way. Finish her off with some flaky sea salt and take a picture because you're def going to want to share this on Instagram.

Schmear a really thick layer of coconut labneh on each piece of toasted bread. Lay the radish slices on top of the labneh. Spoon the peanut salsa over the radish slices. Garnish with cilantro and season with flaky salt and black pepper to taste. Serve immediately. This is best enjoyed right away.

Lumpia Crackers

SERVES 6 TO 8

Kosher salt

Neutral oil, such as canola or grapeseed oil

Twenty-five 8 in [20 cm] spring roll wrappers

1. Line a baking sheet with paper towels and have a bowl of kosher salt near the stove.

2. In a Dutch oven, add oil to a depth of 1 in [2.5 cm]. Turn the heat to medium-high and heat the oil until it registers 350°F [180°C] on a frying thermometer.

3. Using tongs, carefully place one spring roll wrapper in the oil and fry. Push the wrapper down until it turns golden brown, 2 to 3 minutes. Flip the spring roll wrapper and fry for an additional 2 minutes. Transfer the spring roll wrapper to the prepared baking sheet to drain. Immediately season with kosher salt. Repeat with the remaining spring roll wrappers.

4. To serve, pile the lumpia crackers onto a serving platter as high as a skyscraper and serve with dips. Enjoy! Store leftover crackers in an airtight container at room temperature for up to 3 days.

I love snacky things—my true joy is just chomping on chips or crackers or toasted nuts. Anything with a crunch! This is a new way to enjoy my other crispy fave, lumpia. Think of this as a deconstructed lumpia without the filling, taking that exterior wrapper and frying it on its own so it turns into a cracker. These seem really fancy and architectural—often they take on beautiful, dramatic shapes—but they're a pretty low-lift snack to make. Despite their delicate appearance, these are surprisingly robust and can take some substantial dips and sauces. Serve them alongside sautéed vegetables (to really make it lumpia-like) or pile them up on a table with assorted dips—they're definitely a conversation starter!

Shallot Confit *with Creamy Whipped Tofu*

SERVES 4 TO 6

Creamy Whipped Tofu / RECIPE ON PAGE 56

3 to 5 confit shallot pieces plus 1 Tbsp oil from Shallot Confit / RECIPE ON PAGE 64

Freshly ground black pepper

1 lemon

1 Tbsp ABC Sweet Soy Sauce

1 Tbsp finely chopped chives

Spring radishes, crackers, or bread, for serving

If I've said it once, I've said it a thousand times: I'm a dip girlie. Seriously, I could eat dip as a whole meal, just snacking my life away. This is one of my favorite versions, taking the Creamy Whipped Tofu (page 56) and topping it with Shallot Confit (page 64). Honestly, if you already have the shallot confit done, this recipe is more about assembling than actual cooking. It's almost like if adobo and French onion dip had an illegitimate baby—in other words, delicious!

To me, this is an all-seasons dip. You can make this any time of year and people will lose their minds. Serve it with crackers, lumpia, Lumpia Crackers (page 140), a fresh crusty loaf of bread, or fresh raw vegetables, like celery, snap peas, or some radishes . . . seriously, it goes with everything!

1. In a serving bowl, with a clean spoon, pile the whipped tofu high like a cloud and create a well in the center. Using another clean spoon, transfer the confit shallots to the well of the tofu. Spoon the shallot oil in with the shallots. The oil should create a pool for the confit shallots to swim in, and it's totally OK if the oil oozes out to the sides of the tofu.

2. Using a pepper grinder, grind the hell out of the pepper over the top of the shallots and tofu. The dip should be blanketed with fresh black pepper. Using a Microplane, zest the lemon and drizzle the sweet soy sauce right over the dip. Shower it with the chives. Serve with an abundance of spring radishes, crackers, or bread. Whatever edible vessel to scoop up the dip!

Gem Lettuce *with Coconut Green Goddess Dressing*

SERVES 4

5 heads little gem lettuce, halved lengthwise

2 tsp extra-virgin olive oil

Zest and juice of 1 lemon

2 tsp kosher salt

1 cup [240 ml] Coconut Green Goddess Dressing / RECIPE ON PAGE 44

¼ cup [5 g] dill

¼ cup [5 g] parsley leaves

5 ramps or green onions, thinly sliced on a bias

Seedy Coconut Confetti / RECIPE ON PAGE 60

This is such a lovely, charming salad—I love how simple it is, which is something you can get away with in the spring. The real MVP is the Coconut Green Goddess Dressing, which I make with coconut milk so there's a hint of tropical atmosphere in there, plus a kick from the jalapeño and herbiness from the dill and parsley. Oh, and then the Seedy Coconut Confetti adds the perfect amount of bite to finish her off. That, with the freshness of the greens, and it delivers on the spring trifecta I'm always looking to create: crunchy, crispy, creamy. The three *C*s are all you need, baby!

1. In a large bowl, add the lettuce. Lubricate them with the olive oil, lemon zest, and lemon juice. Season with the salt and toss well.

2. Arrange the lettuce on a platter. Drizzle the dressing over the lettuce, then nonchalantly scatter the dill, parsley, and ramps on top of the lettuce. Sprinkle with the seedy coconut confetti for a happy ending! This is best enjoyed right away.

Bok Choy and Purple Daikon Salad

SERVES 4

1 lb [455 g] baby bok choy

1 purple daikon radish

1 cup [20 g] cilantro leaves

1 cup [20 g] mint leaves

Pancit Dressing / RECIPE ON PAGE 52

1 Tbsp Seedy Coconut Confetti / RECIPE ON PAGE 60

1. Trim the bottom of the bok choy and separate the leaves. Rinse the bok choy under cold water to remove any dirt. Pat dry with a paper towel. Leave the bok choy leaves whole.

2. Peel the daikon radish and thinly slice on a mandoline or with a sharp knife into slices about ⅛ in [4 mm] thick.

3. Transfer the bok choy, radish, and ½ cup [10 g] of the cilantro leaves and ½ cup [10 g] of the mint leaves to a large bowl. Pour the pancit dressing over the top and toss everything together using tongs until the dressing has coated the salad thoroughly.

4. Transfer the salad to a platter. Rain the remaining cilantro and mint on top of the salad and sprinkle with the seedy coconut confetti. Chow down! This is best enjoyed right away.

First, this salad is STUNNING to look at—the very embodiment of spring with its dazzling green and purple colors. It's such a verdant, kaleidoscopic way to embrace the season. Spring is all about freshness and crunch to me—a reminder that everything is being reborn after a time of hibernation—and this light and lovely salad is the perfect representation of that ethos. Here, I suggest getting a thick, sturdy bok choy that will stand up to the dressing and give you plenty to chomp on. The daikon will add just the right amount of clean, spicy bite that will play off the bok choy.

As for the topping, if you're not a cilantro lover, we can't be friends and you're missing out on one of life's true pleasures—KIDDING!!! Those averse to cilantro can sub in dill; it will provide that herbaceous flavor profile and even add a little bit of an unexpected pickle-y flavor to the proceedings.

Hot Baby Bok Choy

SERVES 4

2 Tbsp unrefined coconut oil

1 lb [455 g] bok choy or baby bok choy

Kosher salt

Freshly ground black pepper

1 lime

2 Tbsp Seedy Chili Oil / RECIPE ON PAGE 56

On page 147, I use a sturdy bok choy as the base of a salad, but here, it's seared. When you cook a green like bok choy, you get this sizzling, charred, caramelized element that is just so damn good. Drizzle it with my Seedy Chili Oil, which has a sneaky coconut flavor—and boom, you've got a really unique side dish that honors the spring season. I love treating the bok choy in a different way than you're used to seeing. She's a versatile gal! She's hot, she's unexpected. Embrace her.

1. Set a sauté pan or cast-iron skillet over medium heat and add the coconut oil.

2. Once the oil is glistening and shimmering, add the bok choy to the pan and season with salt and pepper. Cook for 2 to 3 minutes, then flip and season the other side with salt and pepper. Cook for 2 to 3 minutes more until slightly wilted and certain areas of the leaves have achieved a blotchy caramelized color.

3. Transfer the bok choy to a plate and zest the lime over the top. Cut the lime in half and squeeze the juice over the bok choy.

4. Spoon the chili oil over the bok choy and enjoy! Store leftovers in an airtight container in the refrigerator for up to 3 days.

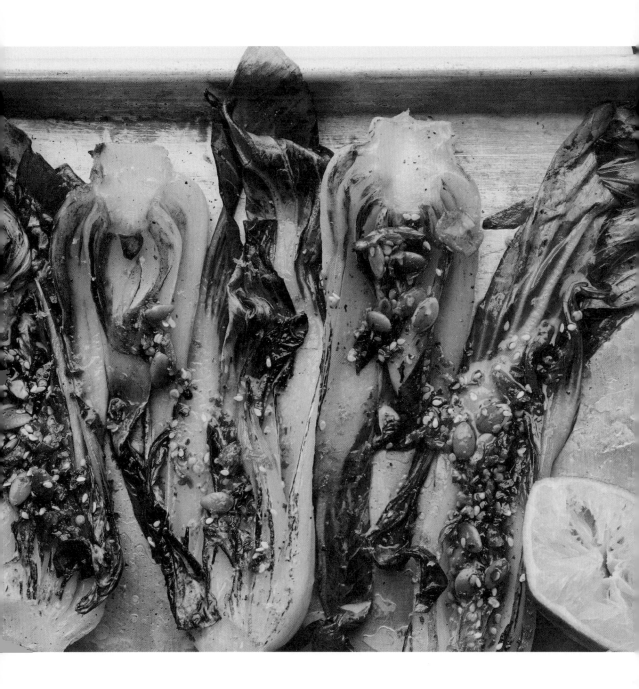

Pancit

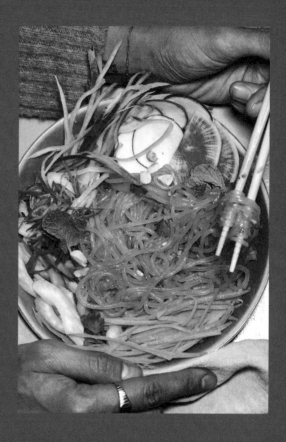

Pancit is a catchall term for stir-fried noodles, but there are a million ways to spin these in different directions. They're usually served with pan-fried vegetables, a protein, and a sauce, but from there, they can be prepared in a variety of ways. The classic version is usually vermicelli rice noodles, but it's totally acceptable to use udon or soba or glass noodles. You can use whatever vegetables are in season, though cutting them up into small pieces is key so they flash fry quickly. And while most people would usually use an animal protein, I often skip it, as it's pretty filling without. Add tofu or beans if you want to amp up the protein.

To me, it's all about the sauce—in the Sawsawsan chapter, you'll find a few sauces that could dress up a pancit dish, but the go-to is the Pancit Dressing on page 52. It's the perfect salty, sweet, hot, sour, umami, oily sauce that will coat the noodles and veggies and bring the dish together.

Pancit Salad

SERVES 4

Kosher salt

1 lb [455 g] sweet potato noodles

2 Tbsp neutral oil, such as canola or grapeseed oil

½ cup [60 g] shredded carrots

½ cup [30 g] thinly sliced red radishes

½ cup [60 g] thinly sliced celery, on a bias

½ cup [10 g] cilantro leaves

5 ramps or green onions [50 g], thinly sliced on a bias

Pancit Dressing / RECIPE ON PAGE 52

⅓ cup [40 g] unsalted peanuts, toasted and chopped

¼ cup [5 g] mint leaves

This is a riff on the Korean noodle dish japchae, and it's all about exciting, enticing textures. First, there's the firm yet slinky sweet potato noodles. Then the pancit dressing, which slides and glides all over the noodles and makes them slippery and wild. I love the slight chew to the noodles too, and the fresh, crunchy vegetables for some textural contrast. The peanuts on top add a dry crunch, and the whole thing is like a spring fling orgy in your mouth. I love it.

Ramps are a type of green onion that only appear for a short time in the spring. In New York, where I live, suddenly there are ramps on every menu for a few weeks, and it's fun to see how people use them. If you can get your hands on some, you absolutely must incorporate them and their delicate yet pungent qualities into this noodle salad. It will just be this heavenly, garlicky, herby addition that will have people swooning, I swear.

1. Bring a large pot of salted water to a boil over medium-high heat. Add the noodles and cook for 5 to 7 minutes. Place a colander in the sink and drain the noodles. Rinse the noodles in cold water for about 3 minutes and drain completely.

2. Transfer the noodles to a large bowl, drizzle with the oil, and toss to prevent the noodles from sticking together. With kitchen scissors, snip into the bowl and cut the noodles into approximately 6 in [15 cm] strips. Add the carrots, radishes, celery, cilantro, and ramps. Pour in the pancit dressing and toss everything together with tongs until well combined.

3. Transfer the noodles to a serving platter and sprinkle the peanuts over the top. Accessorize with the mint leaves and enjoy! Store leftovers in an airtight container in the refrigerator for up to 3 days.

Crispy Lemon Dill Rice

SERVES 4

3 cups [540 g] Stovetop Jasmine Rice / RECIPE ON PAGE 75

1 cup [20 g] chopped dill, plus some whole dill leaves for garnish

2 tsp kosher salt

2 Tbsp avocado oil

2 Tbsp unsalted butter

2 lemons

Flaky sea salt

1. In a medium bowl, mix the rice, ½ cup [10 g] of the chopped dill, and the kosher salt with a wooden spoon or your good old clean hands. Set aside.

2. In a large nonstick pan over medium heat, add the oil and 1 Tbsp of the butter. Swirl the butter until it's completely melted in with the oil and the oil starts to shimmer.

3. Place the rice into the pan and, using a rubber spatula, press the rice down evenly. Cook for about 3 minutes until the rice has a nice golden-brown bottom. Using a butter knife, take the remaining 1 Tbsp butter and rim the edge of the pan to give the rice the extra fat she deserves. Let the rice crisp up for about 5 minutes.

4. To transfer the crispy rice, grab a round platter and place it right on top of the pan. Using a dry kitchen towel, hold the handle of the pan and quickly invert the rice onto the platter. Remove the pan and it should reveal a glowy and crispy giant rice cake!

5. Take a Microplane and zest one lemon over the crispy rice. Cover the rice with the remaining ½ cup [10 g] of dill, then cut the lemon in half and squeeze the juice right on top of the dill and rice. Thinly slice the second lemon and remove the seeds. Scatter the lemon slices on top of the rice. Finish her off with flaky salt and enjoy! Store leftover rice in an airtight container in the refrigerator for up to 3 days.

I would gladly bet my life's savings that if you walked into any Asian household, they have a bowl or pot of leftover rice in the fridge. It was like this in my home growing up, and it's like this in any respectable Asian household. This is my proposal for turning that day-old grain into an exciting stand-alone dish.

The key is to really sear the dried-out rice to turn it into an oversized crispy rice cake that you can break apart. The lemon and dill give it some vernal flavor. I just love the bright acidity of lemon and the anisey taste of dill; together they really play up that spring vibe and pair well with the crunchy charred yumminess of the rice. This is a great side dish with a protein, but honestly, I happily eat this on its own.

Mushroom Bulaklak *with Coconut Hot Sauce*

SERVES 4

FOR FRYING
Neutral oil, such as canola or grapeseed oil
1 lb [455 g] oyster mushrooms

WET BATTER
One 14 oz [420 ml] can unsweetened coconut milk
1 Tbsp garlic powder
1 tsp kosher salt
1 tsp white pepper

DRY BATTER
1 cup [135 g] rice flour
1 cup [180 g] potato starch
1 Tbsp kosher salt
1 Tbsp white pepper
1 Tbsp garlic powder

FOR SERVING
Kosher salt
Coconut Hot Sauce / RECIPE ON PAGE 45

1. TO FRY: Line a plate with paper towels. Fill a large, heavy-bottom pot or Dutch oven about halfway with oil and warm over medium-high heat until the oil reaches 350°F [180°C].

2. Trim off the tough ends of the oyster mushrooms. Using your hands, gently pull apart the mushrooms into small clusters.

3. TO MAKE THE WET BATTER: In a large bowl, add the coconut milk and whisk in the garlic powder, salt, and white pepper.

4. TO MAKE THE DRY BATTER: In a separate large bowl, whisk together the rice flour, potato starch, salt, white pepper, and garlic powder.

5. Working in batches, coat the mushrooms with the wet batter and toss them in the dry batter. Make sure the mushrooms are evenly coated and shake off any excess batter. Fry them in the hot oil until golden brown, 3 to 5 minutes. Carefully use a spider or slotted spoon to transfer the fried mushrooms to the paper towel–lined plate and season with salt immediately. Serve right away, hot or at room temperature, along with coconut hot sauce for dipping.

Growing up, I vividly remember my dad and his friends hanging in the backyard at a round table playing mah-jongg. They would play for hours and sip on cold cans of Budweiser and nibble on a plateful of fried, fatty, salty chicharon bulaklak with a vinegar dipping sauce. Chicharon bulaklak are fried ruffles of pork fat, a popular, indulgent, and crispy Filipino street food. I wanted to re-create this delectable treat with a vegetarian spin: Instead of ruffles of pork fat, I use ruffles of oyster mushrooms. Full-fat coconut milk acts as a coating to replicate the fattiness from the pork. The oyster mushrooms are fried to golden-brown, crunchy morsels and served with my Coconut Hot Sauce. It's the perfect modern Filipino appetizer.

Asparagus Lumpia *with Herby Fish Sauce*

SERVES 6 TO 8

25 large asparagus spears

Twenty-five 8 in [20 cm] spring roll wrappers

Neutral oil, such as canola or grapeseed oil, for frying

Kosher salt

Large head red lettuce, leaves separated, for serving

Fresh mint, for serving

Cilantro, for serving

Herby Fish Sauce / RECIPE ON PAGE 49, for serving

1. Line a baking sheet with paper towels.

2. Trim the woody bottoms of the asparagus.

3. Gently peel apart the spring roll wrappers and work with one wrapper at a time. Keep the reserved wrappers covered with a damp cloth or in the plastic wrapper.

4. On a clean, flat surface, place a wrapper with the flat side facing you. Place an asparagus spear horizontally on the bottom of the wrapper (it's OK if the asparagus is a little longer or shorter than the wrapper; these don't have to look perfect to taste good!). Roll the wrapper up like a joint, leaving about a 1 in [2.5 cm] overhang at the top. With your clean fingertips, dab water on the overhang and continue rolling to seal the lumpia. Transfer the lumpia seam side down to the paper towel–lined baking sheet and cover with a damp cloth. Repeat with the remaining asparagus and spring roll wrappers.

5. In a high-sided, heavy-bottom pan, pour in 2 to 3 in [5 to 7.5 cm] of oil. Heat the oil over medium-high heat for about 7 minutes, or until it reads 350°F [180°C] on a frying thermometer.

6. Working in batches, fry 3 to 5 lumpia, making sure not to overcrowd the pan. Fry each side for 3 to 5 minutes until crispy and a sensual golden-brown color. Transfer the lumpia back onto the paper towel–lined baking sheet and immediately season with salt.

7. To serve, arrange the lumpia, lettuce, mint, and cilantro on a platter. Pour the herby fish sauce into a small sauce bowl and snuggle it in on the platter. To eat, wrap the lumpia with the lettuce and herbs, dunk it into the sauce, and inhale it! These are best enjoyed right away.

Real talk—this is about as easy as a recipe gets. Wrap a piece of asparagus in a lumpia wrapper and fry it. And it makes the perfect little springtime crunchy snack that you can munch on before dinner (or during dinner! Or after dinner!). And while the freshness of the asparagus and the naughty crunch of the fried wrapper are a great pair, add in a sweet-spicy-herby sauce, and this is heaven. People will be crowding around this plate all night, for real. Here's a little tip: Make more than you think you need because they will go way more quickly than you expect.

Miso Sinigang

SERVES 6

2 Tbsp avocado oil

1 small yellow onion, sliced

4 garlic cloves, finely chopped

1 Tbsp grated fresh ginger

3 Tbsp reduced sodium miso paste

2 Tbsp tamarind concentrate

2 Tbsp fish sauce

1 Tbsp lemongrass powder, preferably Burlap and Barrel

2 cups [120 g] shiitake mushrooms, thinly sliced

One 14 oz [400 g] block firm tofu, cut into small cubes

Kosher salt

Freshly ground black pepper

4 oz [115 g] fresh spinach

1 small green radish, thinly sliced

Stovetop Jasmine Rice / RECIPE ON PAGE 75, for serving

This is my riff on sinigang, a traditional pork and vegetable soup that's very sour-forward and was a staple in my house growing up. I swap out the meatiness of pork ribs for earthy shiitake mushrooms and tofu to give my version of this comforting soup more substance. The tart flavor comes from tamarind paste, and I've added miso, which is not usually in the soup but creates a base of rich, umami flavor to counterbalance the mouth-puckering tartness. Adding in fresh spinach at the end gives her the grassy, fresh spring flair that I truly love leaning into this time of year. Plus it's a nice way to get in some greens. Pair the soup with steamed jasmine rice and you've got yourself a full meal.

1. In a large Dutch oven over medium heat, warm the avocado oil. Add the onion, garlic, and ginger. Sauté for 2 to 3 minutes. Add 5 cups [1.2 L] of water and whisk in the miso, tamarind, fish sauce, and lemongrass powder. Bring to a simmer and cook for 10 minutes.

2. Add the mushrooms and tofu. Decrease the heat to low and gently cook for 7 to 10 minutes more.

3. Season with salt and pepper to taste. Remove from the heat and add the spinach and radish. Divide the soup among six bowls and serve with rice.

4. To store, let the soup cool to room temperature. Transfer to an airtight container and store in the refrigerator for up to 3 days.

Vegan Bibingka

MAKES ONE 9 IN [23 CM] ROUND CAKE

1¼ cups [170 g] rice flour

1¼ cups [165 g] glutinous rice flour

1 cup [200 g] sugar

1 Tbsp baking powder

1 tsp kosher salt

One 14 oz [420 ml] can unsweetened coconut milk

1 cup [240 g] coconut yogurt

½ cup [110 g] unrefined coconut oil, melted

½ cup [120 ml] seltzer water

1 tsp vanilla extract

1. Preheat the oven to 350°F [180°C] and position the rack in the middle of the oven. Spray a 9 by 2 in [23 by 5 cm] round cake pan with nonstick canola cooking spray.

2. In a large bowl, whisk together the rice flour, glutinous rice flour, sugar, baking powder, and salt.

3. In a medium bowl, whisk together the coconut milk, coconut yogurt, melted coconut oil, seltzer water, and vanilla. Whisk the wet ingredients into the dry ingredients until the mixture is fully incorporated and the batter is smooth.

4. Pour the batter into the prepared cake pan and bake for 1 hour, or until a wooden skewer inserted into the center comes out clean.

5. Let the bibingka cool completely in the pan. After the cake is cool, slide a butter knife around the sides of the pan to release the cake from the pan. Gently invert the cake onto a serving plate or cake stand. Store covered at room temperature for up to 3 days.

For a while, my friend chef Tara Thomas had been asking me to make a vegan version of bibingka. During the pandemic, when I was living upstate and didn't have a ton to do, I decided to dive in. I really had to work hard on this, which was a surprise because bibingka already uses coconut milk—all you really have to do is swap the eggs out. But the first time I made it, it was just FINE. Boo. So I kept chipping away at it, and slowly fine-tuned the recipe. Now I finally understand her (and by *her*, I mean the bibingka). She's finicky and, because every oven isn't so forgiving, you've really got to stay focused and keep your head in the game to achieve that glowy, golden, sun-kissed hue. But lucky for you, I now have a beautiful vegan alternative. And, yes, Tara loved it and appreciated all my hard work.

Summer

Summer Is a Party,
Summer Is Casual,
Summer Is Abundance

I adore summer—how can you not? But there are two things, for me, that make it so special. First, it's a season of celebration, and second, it's hands-down the sexiest time of year.

For me, there's this especially strong sense of celebration during this time of year. That's mostly because me, my twin brother, my older brother, and my grandmother all celebrate our birthdays over July and August.

My main summer memory as a kid is a big birthday party in August, filled with family, friends, and lots of food and action. It was Leo season, a time of being bold, confident, and the center of attention, which resonated with me. The house was taken over, with people spilling into every room, the garage, and the backyard. It was loud, and everyone really let loose.

Some things stand out in my memory: people yelling at the TV as they watched sports, my aunt playing the piano while we all gathered around and sang Filipino songs, and my lola sharing stories about when she was a beauty queen back home—again, loudly. My grandma would show me pictures of her on a throne wearing a tiara and a traditional Filipino dress with these bold, circular shoulders (the dress is known as Filipiniana). I was filled with awe at just how regal and elegant she was. I like to think those qualities trickled down to me and my twin brother—though, honestly, mostly to me.

Food was a huge part of the festivities. My mom would make this refreshing melon juice and we'd have a whole roast pig on a buffet table. The best part—the piece that everyone would fight over—was the crispy, fatty skin. My mouth waters just thinking about it. The cooks in the family would make this all-purpose sauce using the pig's organs smashed together and mixed with brown sugar. It's divine.

It was really wild and fun, and the whole house was taken over by people. Everyone had a role to play, and I would watch it all unfold. So many gifts! So much love! It was a sensory experience: the heat of the day slowly fading after the sun went down;

the loud sounds of laughter, singing, and people in passionate conversations; music playing; strong aromas floating from the kitchen or the backyard—the works! It was the sound of family, of life.

Now, as an adult, I love summer for different reasons. Mainly, it's just a really alluring, super sexy time of year. Everything about summer has this sensual undertone, especially the food. The way it feels to bite into a fleshy stone fruit like a peach or plum and have the juice drip down your chin. The refreshing crispness of a cucumber, colorful berries, sticky hands, flickering candles on an al fresco table, sweaty skin, a little stain of fruit juice on a crisp cotton shirt, eating something cold in a damp swimsuit, tanned skin contrasted against a white tee—all of these are my grown-up memories of summer.

In summer, I honor Mother Nature by keeping things simple and celebrating the purity of natural flavors and textures. On hot days, it's more about arranging ingredients with minimal fuss, letting their flavors sing. While grilling is great, sometimes just arranging beautiful greens or fruits can tell the season's story. I aim for a casual, leisurely, thrown-together elegance in my meals.

The first time I went to Fire Island I saw just how summer intoxicates people—they become wild and carefree, this different version of themselves. It's a reflection of the wildness and abundance of the earth during this season. I don't think it's an accident that Pride Month is June. That feeling of both celebration and nonchalance really sets the tone for the season. Any time I cook in the summer, I try to capture that feeling, and I hope these recipes express that.

Melon Juice

SERVES 4

SIMPLE SYRUP
½ cup [100 g] sugar

MELON JUICE
1 firm cantaloupe
3 cups [720 ml] filtered water
½ cup [120 ml] unsweetened coconut milk
¼ cup [60 ml] tequila or Aplós Arise (optional)
Handful fresh mint leaves, plus more for garnish

You know those summer days where it's just so swampy and hot out and your body feels so, so heavy? And you're just sticky and gross and you want something refreshing and thirst-quenching, and (sorry!) water just ain't cutting it? Enter Melon Juice. It's stunningly simple, yet it packs some serious punch in conquering the sweltering heat that hangs in the air during those dog days of summer. That's when melons are the juiciest and ripest and begging to be turned into something restorative and invigorating. Both my mom and lola made this when I was young, and now I do the same but with my own spin. And there's just something so sensory and fun about it: the milky, opaque juice with flecks of orange melon, the way it instantly cools your body down on that very first sip. Often the melon pulp has a squiggly shape and (I don't know how else to put it) it makes you feel a bit squiggly when you drink it. And while I don't usually add booze to it, as it dilutes the consistency, if you're feeling frisky you could add some tequila or a nonalcoholic spirit like Aplós Arise. Cheers!

NOTE: *Melon scraper* or *pangkayod* is a Filipino term referring to a grater or shredder. It is often employed to grate ingredients like coconut, cheese, vegetables, and for this particular recipe, cantaloupe. The term is derived from the Filipino verb *kayod*, which means "to scrape" or "to grate." This particular tool is also known as a coconut grater.

1. TO MAKE THE SIMPLE SYRUP: In a small saucepan over medium heat, combine the sugar with ½ cup [120 ml] of water. Stir until the sugar has dissolved. Remove from the heat and let cool completely.

2. TO MAKE THE MELON JUICE: Set a fine-mesh sieve over a large bowl. Cut the cantaloupe in half. Using a spoon, remove the pulp and seeds and transfer to the sieve. Gently grind the pulp with the back of a spoon to release the juices into the bowl. Discard the pulp and seeds. Using a melon scraper, scrape all of the melon flesh into the bowl with the juices.

3. Pour the water into the bowl. Stir in the coconut milk, simple syrup, and tequila, if using. Sprinkle in fresh mint. Refrigerate for about 30 minutes.

4. Fill four glasses with ice cubes and pour in the melon juice. Garnish with fresh mint and enjoy! Melon juice is best enjoyed the day it's made.

Stone Fruit *with Coconut Yogurt Cream*

SERVES 4

3 ripe but firm peaches, cut into wedges

3 red plums, cut into wedges

2 cups [340 g] fresh Bing cherries, pitted

Zest and juice of 1 lemon

1 tsp kosher salt

2 Tbsp Coconut Palm Sugar Syrup / RECIPE ON PAGE 68

Coconut Yogurt Cream / RECIPE ON PAGE 69

Handful fresh mint leaves

My tita Becky used to make a fruit salad growing up: canned fruit with its sticky syrup poured over thick, creamy condensed milk all folded together . . . and that's all she wrote! It's a pretty common sweet treat in Filipino households, especially during the warmer months. My version makes use of fresher ingredients and has a slightly lighter touch. I love serving this in August when stone fruits are at their peak. The vibrant colors of their skins and the thick, treacly juices mixing with the fluffy, cloud-like Coconut Yogurt Cream and then the tart sting of cherries and citrus—heaven in a bowl! It's great for a brunch or dessert or even an afternoon snack; there's just something so nostalgic about it.

Often I'll serve it with the cream on the bottom and the fruit tumbled on top, with fresh mint sprigs sprinkled over it. It has a sort of "thrown together but devastatingly chic" vibe to it. Like, *Oh, this old thing? I just tossed it together willy-nilly*. Meanwhile all your friends are taking pictures of it. It's a crowd-pleaser, for sure.

1. In a medium bowl, toss the peaches, plums, cherries, lemon zest, lemon juice, salt, and coconut palm sugar syrup together. Let the fruit sit and play in the bowl for a few moments to gently marinate in the syrup and let the juices from the fruit ooze out.

2. On a serving platter, use a spoon to dollop and smear the coconut yogurt cream to create a cloud for the fruit to rest on.

3. Spoon the fruit onto the bed of the coconut yogurt cream and drizzle the syrup and juices from the bowl on top.

4. Garnish with fresh mint leaves and more lemon zest and indulge! This is best eaten right away.

Summer

Atchara Plate

SERVES 8

Pickled Bitter Melon / RECIPE ON PAGE 62
Pickled Carrots / RECIPE ON PAGE 63
Pickled Green Daikon / RECIPE ON PAGE 63
Pickled Golden Raisins / RECIPE ON PAGE 62

Atchara is pickled papaya, and I credit it for starting my lifelong love of all things pickled. This recipe pumps up the volume by creating a whole platter dedicated to yummy pickled delights: raisins, bitter melon, green daikon, and carrots. Despite them all being pickled, there's a wide variety of flavor profiles represented, from the sweet and juicy raisins to the spicy, peppery daikon. Plate all these little gems together in a lovely spread, and it's like a Filipino-ish take on the classic Italian aperitivo snack. This is for all you summer girlies who like to pick and graze all day—in other words, me!

Place the pickled melon, carrots, and daikon in small bowls, then place on a platter, creating a beautiful arrangement. Fill a small bowl with pickled golden raisins and nestle it in on the platter among the vegetables. Serve to your summer girlies and enjoy!

Summer

Falafel Lumpia

MAKES 25 LUMPIA, SERVES 6 TO 8

Two 15 oz [430 g] cans chickpeas, drained and rinsed

3 garlic cloves, minced

1 small shallot, chopped

1 tsp ground cumin

1 tsp ground coriander

1 tsp Guntur Sannam Chili Powder (Diaspora Co.) or red pepper flakes

1 tsp kosher salt, plus more to taste

1 tsp freshly ground black pepper

½ cup [10 g] parsley leaves

½ cup [10 g] cilantro leaves

1 lemon

3 Tbsp Spicy Miso Tahini / RECIPE ON PAGE 54

¼ cup [60 ml] extra-virgin olive oil

Twenty-five 8 in [20 cm] spring roll wrappers

Neutral oil, such as canola or grapeseed oil, for frying

Sweet and Spicy Banana Ketchup / RECIPE ON PAGE 49, for serving

Whipped Tahini / RECIPE ON PAGE 50, for serving

The idea for this dish came from a pop-up I did with chef Edy Massih of Edy's Grocer, a Lebanese deli in Greenpoint, Brooklyn. The pop-up offered a collaborative menu of Lebanese and Filipino food, in celebration of Asian American and Pacific Islander Heritage month. Honestly, events like this are a reminder of why I love living in New York, and specifically Brooklyn—there are always so many creative, interesting things going on that push you outside of yourself and your comfort zone. So this is me taking something from Middle Eastern cuisine— falafel, a fried chickpea patty—and using it in a signature Filipino dish—lumpia, a crispy, fried spring roll. The result is a small, crunchy snack packed with intoxicating aromatic spices. Which sounds kinda hoity-toity, but the dish is not—it's just, like, an addictively crispy, spice-filled cigar.

1. In the bowl of a food processor, add the chickpeas, garlic, shallot, cumin, coriander, chili powder, salt, pepper, parsley, and cilantro. Pulse a few times, then process until the falafel mixture forms a coarse paste, about 2 minutes. Scrape down the sides of the bowl with a rubber spatula, then squeeze in the juice of the lemon. Add the spicy miso tahini and olive oil. Purée the mixture until a smooth and thick paste forms, about 2 minutes.

continued

2. Scoop the falafel mixture into a big zip-top plastic bag and push the mixture into one of the corners, leaving a space of about 2 in [5 cm] in the corner that you will snip off to pipe out the mixture onto the spring roll wrappers. Squeeze out as many air pockets as you can.

3. Place a small bowl of water near your work station. Line a rimmed baking sheet with paper towels.

4. Peel off 5 spring roll wrappers and lay them on a clean work surface. With a kitchen shear, snip off the corner of the bag and pipe the falafel mixture along the bottom of each sheet. Fill in one end to the other until each sheet is filled. You should be piping about 1½ Tbsp of the filling per wrapper. Roll each wrapper up, leaving 1 in [2.5 cm] at the end. With your clean fingertips, dab water on the overhang of the wrapper and roll to seal the lumpia. Transfer the lumpia seam side down onto the paper towel–lined baking sheet and cover with a damp cloth. Repeat with the remaining filling and wrappers.

5. At this point, you can freeze the lumpia if you are preparing them in advance. Place the lumpia in a single layer on a parchment paper–lined baking sheet; make sure they are not touching so they don't stick to each other. Place the baking sheet uncovered in the freezer for 2 hours until they are firm. Transfer the frozen lumpia to freezer-safe bags. Label the bags with the date and store in the freezer for up to 1 month. To cook frozen lumpia, add 2 to 3 minutes to the frying time.

6. Pour the oil into a high-sided, heavy-bottom pan to a depth of 2 to 3 in [5 to 7.5 cm]. Heat over medium-high heat for about 7 minutes, or until it reads 350°F [180°C] on a frying thermometer.

7. Working in batches, fry 3 to 5 lumpia at a time, making sure not to crowd the pan. Fry each side for 3 to 5 minutes, until crispy and a sensual golden-brown color. Transfer the lumpia to the paper towel–lined baking sheet and immediately season with salt. Transfer to a serving platter and enjoy them with banana ketchup and whipped tahini. These are best eaten right away.

Summer Crudités *with Miso Mushroom Bagoong*

3 baby bok choy, halved lengthwise

3 medium carrots, halved lengthwise

3 Persian cucumbers, quartered lengthwise

1 small bunch French breakfast radishes

2 cups [320 g] cherry tomatoes

1 lb [455 g] small patty pan squash, sliced widthwise

Miso Mushroom Bagoong / RECIPE ON PAGE 54

Maybe this is a weird story, but when my grand-mother passed away, my mother asked me to make something for her wake, and I made crudités. And . . . no one touched it. It's because Filipinos want things to be cooked; they're generally not into raw things (my family was like, "Can we make this into chop suey?" Lol). Needless to say, I was pretty hurt, and so this recipe is like my chance at redemption. Please don't let me fail!

Despite that traumatic experience, I love a crudités plate. Again, why not just serve up fresh, locally sourced vegetables and let their flavor, freshness, and texture really sing? Mother Nature is the best cook out there, after all. However, pairing those veggies with a silky, glossy, flavorful sauce to highlight and punctuate their flavor helps turn up the volume and elevate this dish. Think of the Miso Mushroom Bagoong as some lip gloss for that carrot, babe!

On a serving platter, assemble the vegetables by color in a circle around the edges. In a small saucepan, add the miso mushroom bagoong and warm over low heat until the oil is melted. Pour the warm miso mushroom bagoong into a small serving bowl and place it in the middle of the platter. That's all, period, dot! The miso mushroom bagoong can be prepped 3 days ahead and then reheated to serve warm.

Ensaladang Peach

SERVES 4

3 firm, juicy peaches, pitted and sliced into ¼ in [6 mm] wedges

2 cups [320 g] mixed cherry tomatoes, halved

5 napa cabbage leaves, roughly chopped

½ cup [10 g] dill leaves

Zest of 1 lime

Honey Lime Vinaigrette / RECIPE ON PAGE 51

1 Tbsp sunflower seeds, toasted

This salad was inspired by ensaladang mangga (Filipino mango salad), which consists of the amazing combination of fresh mango, tomato, onion, and vinegar. It packs a juicy, sweet, sharp, pungent punch. Here, in keeping with the season, I traded mangoes for juicy summer peaches and made it heartier with the addition of napa cabbage. It's a crisp and sultry dish, perfect for those steamy summer cookouts.

1. In a large bowl, add the peaches, tomatoes, cabbage, and dill. Add the lime zest and mix the party well.

2. Pour the honey lime dressing over the salad and mix until well combined. Shower the sunflower seeds over the top and enjoy right away! The dressing can be prepped up to 7 days ahead, and the salad can be prepped 1 hour before serving.

Sungold and Pipino

SERVES 4

1 small red onion, thinly sliced

One 2 in [5 cm] piece fresh ginger, peeled and julienned

Vinegar Sauce / RECIPE ON PAGE 52

3 cups [360 g] yellow cucumbers, cut into 1 in [2.5 cm] medallions

4 cups [640 g] Sungold tomatoes, halved

Kosher salt

Freshly ground black pepper

2 Tbsp Pickled Golden Raisins / RECIPE ON PAGE 62

¾ cup [15 g] cilantro leaves, finely chopped

This is my version of a Filipino tomato and cucumber salad that's traditionally served with grilled meats and fish (*pipino* means "cucumber" in Tagalog). I turned up the volume by adding in pops of chewy, pickled golden raisins and using my favorite sweet summer tomato, Sungold. The way it's prepared, it should be thick and chunky, almost like a relish, and it really brightens up whatever it's served with. It's an orgy of flavors and textures, especially that sweet pickled flavor from the raisins, the herbaceous freshness of the cilantro, and the subtle heat of the ginger. In addition to meats and fish, I've served this over hearty vegetable dishes. To be honest, I've even eaten it on crackers and chips—it's that good.

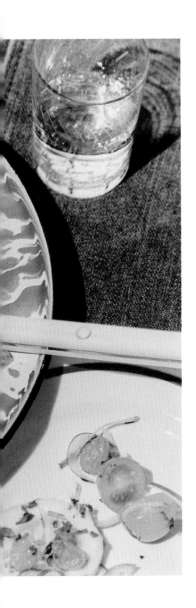

1. In a large bowl, combine the onion, ginger, and vinegar sauce and let sit for 15 minutes.

2. Toss in the cucumbers and tomatoes with the rest of the party crew and hand mix so it all dances together. Season with salt and pepper. Add the raisins, garnish with the cilantro, and serve. This salad can be prepped 1 hour ahead of serving.

Summer

Kamatis *with Herby Fish Sauce*

SERVES 4 TO 6

5 mixed heirloom tomatoes, cut into ½ in [13 mm] wedges

10 Sungold tomatoes, halved

2 Tbsp extra-virgin olive oil

½ cup [10 g] Thai basil leaves

Kosher salt

Freshly ground black pepper

Herby Fish Sauce / RECIPE ON PAGE 49

1 cup [20 g] watercress

½ cup [10 g] dill leaves

¼ cup [50 g] unsalted roasted peanuts, chopped

Other than plums, tomatoes are my favorite summer fruit—they really are the crown jewel of the season. That's why you see a few recipes in this chapter that are centered around them—and not only centered around them, but really focused on accentuating their actual flavor, as opposed to cooking them to alter them from their natural state. This dish is about the tomatoes themselves, and then we add a flavor bomb to sort of highlight them (oh, and P.S., *kamatis* is just Tagalog for "tomato").

I think people are surprised at how yummy this dish is considering it's so straightforward. But there's something so elegant about simplicity, you know? And I recognize some people are wary of fish sauce because it's a bit of a dynamic taste, but all I have to say is, lean into it, babe. If you're afraid of fish sauce, it's time to get over that fear! This dish will definitely help you overcome it.

1. In a large bowl, add the heirloom tomatoes and Sungold tomatoes. Add the olive oil and basil and gently toss to combine. Season with salt and pepper to taste.

2. On a serving platter, scatter the tomatoes. Generously spoon the herby fish sauce right on top of the tomatoes. Sprinkle the watercress, dill, and peanuts over the top. Chow down! This dish can be prepped 1 hour ahead of serving and is best enjoyed the day it's made.

Summer

Adobo

Adobo is probably the number one thing most people think of when they think of Filipino food. Growing up, my grandma made it, my dad made it, my aunts made it; it was always around.

I think the reason adobo is such a signature is because it perfectly encapsulates the essential components of Filipino cooking: garlic, soy sauce, bay leaf, peppercorn, and vinegar, all mixed together in this complex sauce that's just so luxurious. The best part is, if you have the ingredients, it is really easy to make.

Despite it being pretty simple, it creates a nuanced, layered flavor—salty and earthy profiles, balanced with sweet and sour and, underneath, just a touch of spice. It's heaven and really transports me back to my childhood

cooking in the kitchen with my lola or mom. Being in the kitchen with them, I felt loved and grounded. I can vividly remember the scent that my lola would wear—a combination of Johnson & Johnson powder and her favorite flower, sampaguita (jasmine)—mingling with the aromas of adobo simmering in a pot on the stove.

Traditionally, adobo is paired with a meat, but I prefer using it with a vegetable. On page 197, for example, I've used it with green beans, and on page 94 with mushrooms. Mushrooms are an easy substitute because they already have a meat-like texture and take to the sauce really well. Adobo can also work with tofu, seitan, jackfruit, eggplant, or beans. Experiment! Have fun!

Adobo Green Beans

SERVES 4

2 Tbsp avocado or canola oil

1 lb [455 g] green beans

Kosher salt

Freshly ground black pepper

Adobo Vinaigrette / RECIPE ON PAGE 51

1 or 2 green onions, chopped on a bias (about ¼ cup [12 g])

2 tsp pink peppercorns, crushed

There's something so summery to me about charring a vegetable: There's that blackened skin and the smoky flavor that brings to mind a barbecue (though you can also create it in a skillet). Char adds a unique texture and taste that feels very specific to this time of year. Here, I apply that to verdant green beans and then dress them in something light but flavorful to add balance. The adobo vinaigrette coats the beans perfectly and gives them lovely character.

1. In a sauté pan or cast-iron skillet over medium-high heat, add the avocado oil. Once the oil shimmers, add the green beans. Don't mess with it! Let the beans sit so they can achieve the charred and blistered effect, about 4 minutes. After that, wiggle the green beans around the pan until they are cooked, about 6 minutes more. Season with salt and pepper to taste.

2. Transfer the green beans to a serving bowl. Drizzle the adobo vinaigrette over the green beans and gently toss to coat. Scatter the green onions over the green beans and finish them off with a sprinkling of crushed pink peppercorns. Store leftovers in an airtight container in the refrigerator for up 3 days.

Talong *with Seedy Chili Oil*

SERVES 2

1 large Italian eggplant, halved lengthwise

2 tsp sumac

Kosher salt

3 Tbsp avocado oil, plus more as needed

1 lime

Seedy Chili Oil / RECIPE ON PAGE 56

1 Tbsp ABC Sweet Soy Sauce

10 Thai basil leaves

Three words for you: Smoky! Earthy! Juicy! That's what this recipe is all about. And the real magic here is making sure you get a good blackened, blistering, charred skin on that eggplant (psst: *talong* = "eggplant" in Tagalog).

I'll say this: If you're going to do this at home, please make sure you have a strong kitchen fan in place, because, again, smoky burnt eggplant is the goal here. I did this in my Brooklyn apartment and, lord, it was smoke-filled and the fire alarm was going off and . . . it was a bit of a chaotic mess. Even better if you've got access to an outside grill and you can let that smoke be free. Finish her off with some zippy lime, heat, and crunch from the Seedy Chili Oil, floral Thai basil, and sweet soy sauce over caramelized sumac crust. In other words, heaven.

1. Use the tip of a small knife to make small incisions on the interior flesh of the eggplant in a crosshatch pattern. Season abundantly with the sumac and salt.

2. Open your windows and turn your kitchen fan on high. In a sauté pan or cast-iron skillet over medium heat, add the oil. When the skillet is smoking, gently lay the eggplant in the skillet, cut side down. Cook for about 5 minutes until it's charred and caramelized. At this point, your kitchen is probably pretty smoky, which is great for the eggplant! If the pan is looking dry, add 1 to 2 Tbsp of oil to the skillet. Flip the eggplant. Cook for 7 minutes or until the skin of the eggplant has blistered. Remove from the heat and let the eggplant sit in the skillet for 5 minutes.

3. Delicately transfer the eggplant, cut side up, to a plate using tongs. Zest the lime all over the eggplant, then cut the lime in half and squeeze the juice over the eggplant. Spoon the seedy chili oil over everything, filling all of the crevices of the eggplant. Drizzle with the sweet soy sauce, then tear up the basil leaves and let them fall on top of the eggplant. Finito! This is best enjoyed right away.

Oyster Mushroom Skewers *with Mushroom BBQ Sauce*

SERVES 6 TO 8

1½ lb [680 g] oyster mushrooms

Mushroom BBQ Sauce / RECIPE ON PAGE 55

Flaky sea salt

When I think of summer, I think of grilled things on bamboo skewers. For Filipinos, traditionally that means meats—chicken, pork, the usual. I remember growing up, at parties, everyone would walk around with grilled meats on sticks. They're easy to eat at a social event and, let's be honest, grilled things taste great. They're an integral part of summer cooking. I wanted to create a plant-based alternative, so I subbed in oyster mushrooms because they naturally have a really meaty, chewy, fleshy texture. But the secret is really in the sauce. The mushrooms take on its complex, layered flavor beautifully. These skewers are a great way to mix up the go-to summer burger-and-hot-dog repertoire. You won't even miss them, I swear.

1. Soak 6 to 8 bamboo skewers in cold water for 1 hour.

2. Preheat a grill to 400°F [200°C] and oil the grill grate.

3. Pull apart any large pieces of oyster mushrooms into smaller chunks. In a large bowl, add the oyster mushrooms and the mushroom BBQ sauce. Let marinate for 20 minutes.

4. Thread 5 or 6 pieces of mushroom onto each skewer.

5. Grill the mushrooms for 5 minutes on each side until they are charred and caramelized from the mushroom BBQ sauce. Transfer to a platter to serve, and if there's any remaining mushroom BBQ sauce, spoon it all over the grilled oyster mushrooms. Season with flaky salt and voilà! Store leftovers in an airtight container in the refrigerator for up to 3 days.

Plums *with Miso Mushroom Bagoong and Jasmine Rice*

SERVES 2

DRESSING

3 Tbsp extra-virgin avocado oil

2 Tbsp lemon juice

1 Tbsp honey

1 Tbsp pink peppercorns, crushed

1 tsp kosher salt

PLUMS

5 firm plums, cut into wedges

Flaky sea salt

½ cup [10 g] cilantro leaves

½ cup [10 g] Italian parsley leaves

TO SERVE

3 cups [540 g] Stovetop Jasmine Rice / RECIPE ON PAGE 75

Miso Mushroom Bagoong / RECIPE ON PAGE 54

One of my lola's favorite meals was mango with bagoong over rice—simple, delicious, refreshing. It's a perfect summer meal when you're like, "I just don't have it in me to cook right now but I'm hungry." I don't see a ton of mangoes in upstate New York (go figure!) but I do see a lot of plums and pluots, and they have a flavor profile that really complements the bagoong in a way that's similar (sweet) but also distinct (sour). The tart-sweet taste of the plum is a beautiful match for the nutty, earthy umami of the bagoong, and then the rice is just a grounding element that gives it some heft. I have a feeling that once you try this, it will become a go-to summer comfort meal, just like it was for my lola. Sure. Use whatever plums you can find (just know I may be judging you!). I really, really recommend seeking out green plums if you're able; it makes a difference.

1. TO MAKE THE DRESSING: In a medium bowl, whisk together the oil, lemon juice, honey, pink peppercorns, and salt until the honey has dissolved.

2. TO PREPARE THE PLUMS: Add the plums to the bowl with the dressing and toss until they are nicely coated and glossy. Let sit for about 5 minutes. Transfer the plums to a serving plate, sprinkle with flaky salt, and garnish with the cilantro and parsley.

3. TO SERVE: Serve with rice and miso mushroom bagoong. Store leftovers separately in airtight containers in the refrigerator for up to 3 days.

Coconut Herb Rice

SERVES 6

2 cups [400 g] basmati rice, soaked in water for 30 minutes and rinsed

2 cups [480 ml] coconut water

3 cardamom pods

1 star anise

1 bay leaf

1½ tsp kosher salt, plus more to taste

1 Tbsp unrefined coconut oil

Zest and juice of 2 limes

½ cup [75 g] golden raisins

½ cup [50 g] unsalted toasted cashews, roughly chopped

½ cup [10 g] cilantro, chopped

½ cup [10 g] flat-leaf parsley, chopped

1. In a medium saucepan over medium heat, stir together the rice, coconut water, cardamon, star anise, bay leaf, salt, and 1 cup [240 ml] of water. Bring to a boil, then cover and decrease the heat to medium-low. Simmer for 15 to 20 minutes, undisturbed. Turn off the heat and let the rice sit for an additional 10 minutes.

2. Fluff the rice with a fork and stir in the coconut oil. Add the lime zest and juice. Sprinkle in the confetti of raisins, cashews, cilantro, and parsley. Season with salt to taste. Mix the party well and serve! Store leftovers in an airtight container in the refrigerator for up to 3 days.

Obviously, rice is a foundational dish in a lot of cultures. You eat it with pretty much everything, and many Filipino homes have a rice cooker filled with rice at all times. Other recipes in this book call for a more traditional jasmine rice, but for summer, I like a thinner basmati because it yields a drier, looser, more granular rice (jasmine is a bit stickier, which I find to be better for colder months).

I cook this in coconut water and then use coconut oil to really amplify the profile, but to be honest, that flavor is still pretty subtle. What's not subtle are the aromatics (cardamom, star anise, and bay leaf) that perfume the cooked rice. Then we chop up a bunch of lush, verdant herbs and toss them in, which gives it a real "green confetti" vibe, and then add sweet golden raisins for even more pizzazz. Because rice is a supporting player—a side piece, if you will. But, hello, there is a reason we give out Oscars for best supporting actor! The supporting roles are make-or-break (Marisa Tomei in *My Cousin Vinny*, anyone?!), and this is no different. This rice is definitely giving Marisa Tomei.

Banana Ketchup and Tomato Spaghetti

SERVES 4

Kosher salt

1 lb [455 g] spaghetti

¼ cup [60 ml] extra-virgin olive oil

2 Tbsp chili flakes

6 garlic cloves, thinly sliced

4 cups [640 g] mixed cherry tomatoes, stemmed

½ cup [120 ml] banana ketchup

1 cup [20 g] Thai basil

Flaky sea salt, for serving

Sweet spaghetti or Filipino spaghetti is sort of a famous Filipino noodle dish, a type of comfort food that's our riff on bolognese, but made with banana ketchup, which has a sweeter flavor profile. Obviously, summer is lousy with tomatoes, so I thought it would be the perfect time to incorporate fresh tomatoes into a banana ketchup spaghetti–inspired dish. Really, the emphasis is on these sweet Skittles-like mixed cherry tomatoes, which can just burst in your mouth, but when you cook them their skins erupt and they release all these wet, succulent, naughty juices. The result is a really luscious, vibrant, and flavorful sauce that smothers an al dente pasta beautifully. And go heavy on the sauce—this should be a really saucy dish. For me, there's a definite nostalgia factor to this dish, but I've adapted it to my bougie adult life. Plus, it's a way to highlight the fresh ingredients of summer and allow the tomatoes' star quality to shine. She really is an icon, that little fruit!

1. Bring a large pot of salted water to a rolling boil. Add the pasta and cook for about 4 minutes, just shy of al dente. Reserve about 1 cup [240 ml] of the pasta water.

2. In a large saucepan over medium heat, combine the oil, chili flakes, garlic, tomatoes, and banana ketchup. Stir and cook until the tomatoes burst open and their juices ooze out, 6 to 8 minutes. Pour in some of the reserved pasta water, stir, and bring to a gentle simmer. You will notice some of the tomatoes have completely gushed out their juices with their seeds and they are waiting for the strands of pasta to be kissed by them.

3. Toss the pasta into the pool of tomato sauce. Stir the pasta through the sauce and cook for about 3 minutes. Remove from the heat, scatter half of the basil leaves, and lightly toss. Season with kosher salt.

4. Transfer the pasta to a serving platter and garnish with the remaining basil. Sprinkle flaky salt over the top and luxuriate. Store leftovers in an airtight container in the refrigerator for up to 3 days.

Miso Tahini Pancit

SERVES 4

1 lb [455 g] flat rice noodles

1 Tbsp kosher salt

2 Tbsp extra-virgin olive oil

Spicy Miso Tahini / RECIPE ON PAGE 54

1 large cucumber, sliced lengthwise, seeded and diced

1 Tbsp sesame oil

¾ cup [15 g] cilantro, roughly chopped

2 Tbsp Seedy Chili Oil / RECIPE ON PAGE 56

2 Tbsp black sesame seeds

1. Bring a medium pot of water to a boil over medium-high heat.

2. In a large heatproof bowl, add the noodles and season with the salt. Gently pour the boiling water over the noodles. The noodles should be completely submerged in the hot water. Set the bowl aside for 20 minutes. Drain the noodles well, return them to the bowl, and coat with the olive oil. Let them cool completely.

3. Add the spicy miso tahini and toss to coat. Add the cucumber, sesame oil, and cilantro. Drizzle in the seedy chili oil and sprinkle with the black sesame seeds, then she's ready to eat! This is best enjoyed right away.

I just love a cool noodle dish on a humid summer day. (BTW, *pancit* means "noodle" in Filipino; see page 152 for more on pancit.) I first shared this recipe with the brand J.Crew when I modeled for them. Since then, I've evolved the recipe, and I think I really nailed it with the uncomplicated combination of perfectly cooked noodles and creamy dressing. The Spicy Miso Tahini sauce brings a nutty, earthy flavor and a thick creaminess to the dish. I like the simplicity of this recipe, but you could throw in some seasonal veggies such as cucumbers like I did here or green beans to bulk it up (just make sure to chop them bite-size and maybe blanch them first). She's just the perfect side dish, a humble girl, but a beloved one that you won't take for granted.

Summer

Coconut Ice Cream

SERVES 4

One 14 oz [420 ml] can sweetened condensed milk

1 Tbsp vanilla bean paste or vanilla extract

2 cups [480 ml] cold heavy cream

1 tsp kosher salt

12 oz [340 g] macapuno strings, preferably Kamayan

1. Line an 8½ by 4½ in [21.5 by 11 cm] loaf pan with plastic wrap, leaving an overhang of about 3 in [7.5 cm]. Put the pan in the freezer.

2. In a large bowl, add the sweetened condensed milk and stir in the vanilla bean paste. Set aside.

3. In a medium cold metal bowl, add the heavy cream and salt. With a whisk or handheld electric mixer, whisk the cream until it forms billowy peaks.

4. Add ¼ cup [35 g] of the whipped cream to the condensed milk mixture. With a rubber spatula, gently fold it in to incorporate. This will lighten up the condensed milk. Transfer the rest of the whipped cream to the condensed milk and gently fold it in. Mix the macapuno into the cream with the spatula, folding until the mixture is completely smooth and like soft clouds.

5. Transfer the cream to the chilled loaf pan. Smooth out the top with an offset spatula and gently press a piece of wax paper on top of the cream, then fold over the overhanging plastic wrap to secure. Freeze for at least 6 hours to let the ice cream set.

6. To serve, let the ice cream rest at room temperature for about 10 minutes. Remove the plastic wrap and wax paper and scoop to your heart's desire.

7. Store, covered with wax paper and plastic wrap, in the freezer for up to 2 weeks.

I call this "cheater's ice cream" because it gives you that sweet, refreshing, cooling feel of ice cream but without having to get out an ice cream maker and churn and all that. Who has the time? Still, this captures the essence of a great bowl of ice cream, and is even a little lighter, which is great for a really decadent meal when you still want a little happy ending but you're craving something that's not too much of a gut-buster. The little gelatinous, sticky pieces of macapuno give it an additional bit of texture that's surprising and fun. I made this for a dinner party I was hired to cater at Molly Sims's Hamptons house a few summers back, when we were in the midst of "girl dinner," and I have to say, all the girlies were raving about it! So get ready for the compliments.

Lemon Cherry Upside-Down Cake

MAKES ONE 8½ BY 4½ IN [21.5 BY 11 CM] LOAF

CHERRIES

¾ cup [150 g] sugar

2 Tbsp unsalted butter

1 Tbsp lemon juice

1½ cups [250 g] Bing cherries, pitted

CAKE

1 cup [110 g] cassava flour

1 cup [120 g] glutinous rice flour

1 cup [200 g] sugar

1 Tbsp baking powder

1 tsp kosher salt

Zest of 1 lemon

½ cup [110 g] unsalted butter, melted

½ cup [125 g] sour cream

2 eggs, at room temperature

One 14 oz [420 ml] can unsweetened coconut milk

1 tsp vanilla extract

This is a seasonal approach to my dad's favorite cake, which is a pineapple upside-down cake—the classic kind with maraschino cherries on top. My mom would always make it for his birthday, using syrupy canned Dole pineapples.

I kept the cherries but instead of using maraschino, I sub in fresh Bing cherries. Cherries are in abundance during the summer, and they are the perkiest fruit for this cake. I use cassava flour, which is gluten-free but

still yields a really dense and decadent cake. Cassava is actually a root vegetable that is rich in vitamins and minerals, and I remember my mom would use frozen cassava for my dad's cake.

This has been a family tradition for so many years, and it's made me so happy to see that, funnily, upside-down cakes are back. I think the really beautiful, deep bordeaux color from the Bing cherries has such a moody richness and releases such robust flavor—almost like a wine! The cake itself is dense, custardy, and chewy, which is a surprisingly delicious texture that my mom and dad would really enjoy. I consider this a love letter to my parents and their love for each other.

continued

Summer

1. Preheat the oven to 350°F [180°C] and position the rack in the middle of the oven. Spray an 8½ by 4½ in [21.5 by 11 cm] loaf pan with nonstick cooking spray and set it on a baking sheet. (The baking sheet will catch any of the ooziness that spills over from the loaf pan as it bakes.)

2. TO PREPARE THE CHERRIES: In a small saucepan over medium heat, combine the sugar and 3 Tbsp of water. Stir with a rubber spatula and bring to a simmer until the mixture slowly transforms into a caramel-amber color, 5 to 7 minutes.

3. Remove from the heat, add the butter and lemon juice, and whisk until the butter melts. Immediately pour the caramel into the prepared loaf pan. Scatter the pitted cherries evenly over the caramel. Set aside.

4. TO MAKE THE CAKE: In a large mixing bowl, whisk together the cassava flour, glutinous rice flour, sugar, baking powder, salt, and lemon zest.

5. In a separate large mixing bowl, whisk together the melted butter, sour cream, eggs, coconut milk, and vanilla. Pour the wet ingredients into the dry ingredients and whisk until the mixture is fully incorporated and the batter is smooth.

6. Pour the cake batter over the cherries and caramel. Bake for 1 hour and 25 minutes or until a wooden skewer inserted into the center comes out clean. Set the cake on a cooling rack for 30 minutes.

7. Run a butter knife around the sides of the pan, place a platter on top, and invert the cake onto the platter. Slowly remove the cake pan and serve warm or at room temperature. Wrap leftovers tightly in plastic wrap or store in an airtight container at room temperature for up to 3 days.

Blueberry Bibingka

SERVES 6

1¼ cups [170 g] rice flour

1¼ cups [165 g] glutinous rice flour

1 Tbsp baking powder

1 tsp kosher salt

1 cup [200 g] granulated sugar

3 eggs, at room temperature

½ cup [110 g] unsalted butter, melted

One 14 oz [420 ml] can unsweetened coconut milk

1 cup [240 ml] sweetened condensed milk

1 tsp vanilla extract

2 cups [380 g] fresh blueberries

Coconut Yogurt Cream / RECIPE ON PAGE 69, for garnish

It wouldn't be summer without fresh, sweet, stain-your-fingers blueberries! Just imagine driving upstate on a summer day and seeing a roadside farmstand. You pull over, and the first thing that catches your eye are all these pearly, glistening blueberries. Obviously, you immediately know you need to toss those blubies into a bibingka batter and bake it in a cast-iron skillet! No, just me? Well, that was how this cake was born, and the outcome is a gooey, gushy summer snacking cake for those lazy summer mornings.

1. Preheat the oven to 350°F [180°C] and position the rack in the middle of the oven. Spray a 9 in [23 cm] cast-iron skillet with nonstick canola cooking spray and set aside.

2. In a large bowl, whisk together the rice flour, glutinous rice flour, baking powder, and salt.

3. In a medium bowl, whisk together the sugar and eggs. Add the melted butter, coconut milk, sweetened condensed milk, and vanilla. Whisk the wet ingredients into the dry ingredients until the mixture is fully incorporated and the batter is smooth.

4. Pour the batter into the cast-iron skillet. Sprinkle the blueberries over the batter and bake for 1 hour, or until the top and edges are shiny and golden and a wooden skewer inserted into the center comes out clean (other than streaks of blueberry).

5. Let the bibingka cool completely in the pan before serving. Slice the bibingka and serve with a side of coconut yogurt cream. Wrap leftovers tightly in plastic wrap or store in an airtight container at room temperature for up to 3 days.

Strawberry and Coconut Bibingka

MAKES ONE 9 IN [23 CM] ROUND CAKE

BIBINGKA CAKE

1¼ cups [170 g] rice flour

1¼ cups [165 g] glutinous rice flour

1 cup [200 g] sugar

1 Tbsp baking powder

1 tsp kosher salt

One 14 oz [420 ml] can unsweetened coconut milk

½ cup [110 g] unrefined coconut oil, melted

½ cup [120 ml] seltzer water

1 tsp vanilla extract

STRAWBERRY AND COCONUT TOPPING

1 lb [455 g] strawberries, hulled and quartered

Zest and juice of 1 lemon

1 Tbsp sugar

1 tsp sea salt

1½ cups [360 g] Coconut Yogurt Cream / RECIPE ON PAGE 69

This recipe is inspired by one of the most iconic desserts, the strawberry shortcake. I substitute bibingka for the shortcake and swap in coconut yogurt cream for traditional whipped cream, and we get a classic summertime dessert but with a Filipino twist.

I love that this dessert is messy and chaotic. I like to think of it as chaotic abundance, in that you don't want to be too precious with it. It looks best when it has a thrown-together look, a bit haphazard and untidy, with just a small mountain of cream and fruit piled on top of the cake. Not only does it look very cool but it also represents the carefree, laissez-faire energy of summer.

1. **TO MAKE THE BIBINGKA CAKE:** Preheat the oven to 350°F [180°C] and position the rack in the middle of the oven. Spray a 9 by 2 in [23 by 5 cm] round cake pan with nonstick canola cooking spray.

2. In a large bowl, whisk together the rice flour, glutinous rice flour, sugar, baking powder, and kosher salt.

3. In a medium bowl, whisk together the coconut milk, melted coconut oil, seltzer water, and vanilla. Whisk the wet ingredients into the dry ingredients until the mixture is fully incorporated and the batter is smooth.

4. Pour the batter into the prepared cake pan and bake for 1 hour, or until a wooden skewer inserted into the center comes out clean.

5. Let the bibingka cool completely in the pan. After the cake is cool, slide a butter knife down the sides of the pan and slowly move in a circular motion to release the cake from the sides. Gently invert the cake onto a serving plate or cake stand. The cake will keep without the topping wrapped in plastic wrap or stored in an airtight container at room temperature for up to 3 days.

6. **TO MAKE THE STRAWBERRY AND COCONUT TOPPING:** In a large bowl, stir together the strawberries, lemon zest, lemon juice, sugar, and sea salt.

7. With a spoon, spread the coconut yogurt cream evenly on top of the cake. Pile the strawberries over the cream and serve immediately.

Fall

Caterer to
Chef to
Community

If summer meals are about celebration, autumn is a time of community. It's more focused on coziness and building deeper bonds.

Beyond making food, my life as a cook has been about forging strong bonds and creating a community. Food—preparing and eating it—is such a communal, almost sacred act. And while I absolutely love being a cook, it wasn't what I thought I was going to be. I always fantasized about working in fashion, and that's where I started my career, working in magazine publishing and PR. But the kitchen beckoned me, and eventually, I had to answer its call. Even as a little kid, I loved cooking shows and would hang out in the kitchen with the cooks in my family, plus I loved to read cookbooks. So I guess it was always there in the back of my mind. But still, sometimes I look up and see all the pots and pans and ingredients strewn about the counters and am genuinely surprised that this is how I make my living.

And notice I don't say "chef"—that's because I never trained to do this. Not that I'm embarrassed by that fact (after all, neither did Nigella Lawson, a huge hero of mine, and she's doing just fine). I got my start in the less-glamorous world of catering (as opposed to some fancy restaurant), and I fell in love immediately because it was there that I found my community. And community has really been an instrumental, foundational part of this cooking journey for me. It's what fuels me.

When I started making the transition to cooking, I worked in a communal commercial kitchen in Brooklyn with other start-up food businesses, many of them owned and operated by women. It was there, watching and working alongside these female entrepreneurs, that I started to understand the rhythms and realities of a life in the kitchen: how to create food for special occasions and for large groups, how to make things both beautiful and delicious that help foster enduring memories through moments of celebration and joy. As a caterer, you're asked to be a crucial part of these significant times, and that's not a responsibility I take lightly.

It was also during this time that I started to understand how food builds community. As a queer person, I can find working with straight, cis men to be intimidating (think of all the yelling in *The Bear*—not my vibe). But these women were so nurturing and maternal in the way they helped me find my voice through cooking. Their feminine touch gave me confidence and, I think, it allowed me to then embrace a certain feminine energy in my own cooking—emphasizing flavors that were floral and ethereal, or creating dishes that looked delicate and graceful (no slabs of bloody meat here!). Through their support, I was able to be bolder and trust my own instincts. I have these memories of being in that kitchen with them, the sounds and smells, feeling the energy flowing. It was then I started to understand who I was as a cook, as a person, and began seeing these aspects of myself that I had thought of as differences as strengths. I started leaning into my own queerness, my own disability, and my own identity, putting those parts of myself into the food. And suddenly, the dishes felt so personal and alive, and I couldn't wait to share them.

Another reason why I don't love the idea of being a chef is because a chef is such a stand-alone idea. A cook works with a team, in tandem with people. As they say, it takes a village, and it does. It takes a group of people to make a dish, and, often, the best dining experiences are group ones, building relationships over a hot plate or a cold drink. Cooking for people is one beautiful thing, but eating with a group of old friends, new friends, and future friends . . . there's nothing better.

Fall can be bittersweet with summer ending and days getting shorter, but it also brings comfort and security. It's a time to ground oneself with hearty root vegetables and robust, earthy flavors. I enjoy serving roasted vegetables and nourishing stews, lighting candles, and spending cozy evenings with friends. Fall is for rest, renewal, and building community, and I hope these recipes help you embrace that.

Coconut Chia Seed Custard

SERVES 4

2 cups [480 g] coconut yogurt

¼ cup [60 ml] unsweetened coconut milk

2 Tbsp Coconut Palm Sugar Syrup / RECIPE ON PAGE 68

1 tsp vanilla extract

½ cup [90 g] chia seeds

1 tsp kosher salt

Rose Goldenberries / RECIPE ON PAGE 61, for serving

Fresh fruit, for garnish

OK, look, at the end of the day this is, in fact, a chia seed pudding. But I'm a bougie bitch, so I'm calling it a ~custard~ because that sounds fancy, and this is my book and I can do what I want. But seriously, this is a great little on-the-go breakfast or afternoon snack that's light, lovely, and super flavorful. You can make it ahead of time, dollop some fresh fruit on it, and serve. People will just swoon over it, I promise. I started perfecting it in my days as a caterer when I needed a breakfast that was easy and portable but also super delicious and easily digestible. Voilà, this is it! It's pretty healthy, if you're into that, with the sweetness coming from coconut palm sugar, and I really leaned into the island-y coconut flavors. I like that it's filling but not heavy, because no one's trying to start the day so full you want to take a nap at 10 a.m.

1. In a medium bowl, whisk together the coconut yogurt, coconut milk, coconut palm sugar syrup, and vanilla. Stir in the chia seeds and salt. Transfer the chia seed custard to a 32 oz [960 ml] airtight container and refrigerate overnight. Store in the refrigerator until ready to serve and up to 7 days.

2. To serve, divide the chia seed custard among four small bowls, spoon the rose goldenberries on top of each bowl, garnish with fresh fruit, and enjoy.

Fall

Bibingka Waffles

SERVES 4 TO 6

1 cup [135 g] rice flour

1 cup [120 g] glutinous rice flour

½ cup [100 g] sugar

½ cup [50 g] unsweetened coconut flakes

1 Tbsp baking powder

1 tsp kosher salt

One 14 oz [420 ml] can unsweetened coconut milk

3 eggs, at room temperature

1 tsp vanilla extract

Coconut yogurt, fresh fruit, and toasted unsweetened coconut flakes, for serving

1. In a large bowl, whisk together the rice flour, glutinous rice flour, sugar, coconut flakes, baking powder, and salt.

2. In a medium bowl, whisk together the coconut milk, eggs, and vanilla until combined. Whisk the wet ingredients into the dry ingredients until the mixture is fully incorporated and the batter is smooth.

3. Heat a Belgian or standard waffle iron and lightly coat it with nonstick canola cooking spray. Pour ½ to ¾ cup [120 to 180 ml] of batter onto the waffle iron. Cook until crisp and light golden, 5 to 8 minutes. Repeat with the remaining batter.

4. Serve the waffles warm, topped with coconut yogurt, fresh fruit, and toasted coconut flakes.

Growing up, Eggo waffles were not something we had at home, so I always coveted the Eggos that my peers ate for breakfast. When I was invited to cook at a pop-up at my friend's Brooklyn restaurant, I figured it was the perfect opportunity for me to reclaim waffles and make my own version! The rice flour is the secret to these waffles' spongy chew. Top them with fresh fruit, toasted coconut flakes, and coconut yogurt.

Chickpea Sisig Hash

SERVES 2

SISIG SAUCE
2 Tbsp tamari
2 Tbsp Miso Mushroom Bagoong / RECIPE ON PAGE 54
Juice of 1 lime
1 tsp sugar

CHICKPEA HASH
2 Tbsp extra-virgin olive oil
1 small red onion, diced small
3 garlic cloves, minced
1 jalapeño, seeded and diced small
1 red bell pepper, diced
One 15 oz [425 g] can chickpeas, drained
3 green onions, cut on a bias, for garnish

TO SERVE
Stovetop Jasmine Rice / RECIPE ON PAGE 75
2 large eggs, fried sunny-side up

1. TO MAKE THE SISIG SAUCE: In a small bowl, whisk together the tamari, miso mushroom bagoong, lime juice, sugar, and 2 Tbsp of water. Set aside.

2. TO MAKE THE CHICKPEA HASH: In a sauté pan or cast-iron skillet over medium heat, heat the olive oil. Add the onion and sauté for 3 to 4 minutes until translucent. Add the garlic, jalapeño, and bell pepper and sauté for 3 minutes. Add the chickpeas and stir. Cook for 6 to 7 minutes, stirring occasionally, until the chickpeas get slightly browned, crunchy, and slightly soft on the inside.

3. Turn the heat to low and pour in the sisig sauce. Stir completely to get the chickpeas nicely lubricated and cook for an additional 3 minutes. Remove the skillet from the heat. Sprinkle the green onions over the top and enjoy with rice. To go the extra mile, fry up eggs and slide them right over the hash and you got yourself a hearty dish!

4. Store leftover hash (without the fried eggs) in an airtight container in the refrigerator for up to 3 days.

Sisig is a classic Filipino dish made of chopped meat—most often pork bits, like belly and jowl, and chicken liver. It's very textural, unctuous, and indulgent, and it's sometimes served with a fried egg on top. Here, I sub in Miso Mushroom Bagoong for that same meaty texture and then use chickpeas to give it that chopped-up look and mouthfeel. You could add the egg on top here too, for some richness, or serve it with a side of jasmine rice. Either way, this dish really packs a punch.

Ukoy Vegetable Fritter

SERVES 4 TO 6

1 cup [100 g] grated acorn squash

1 cup [100 g] grated sweet potato

1 cup [100 g] grated carrots

1 cup [75 g] sliced green onions

1 cup [115 g] chickpea flour

¼ cup [35 g] rice flour

1 tsp kosher salt, plus more for seasoning

1 cup [240 ml] seltzer water

2 cups [480 ml] neutral oil, such as canola or grapeseed oil

Dill leaves, for garnish

Cilantro leaves, for garnish

Vinegar Sauce / RECIPE ON PAGE 52, for serving

Ukoy (pronounced OO-koy, not YOU-koy) is another classic Filipino dish, a fried vegetable fritter made with shrimp. Think of it like a Filipino latke. And that's exactly how I'm using it here, with autumnal vegetables as the base (sometimes we use bean sprouts and cabbage). It's a great little appetizer, a fun finger food for a special occasion, especially because pan-frying things can be a whole process but yields the perfect snacky hors d'oeuvre. If you want to be fancy about it, you can top it with some crème fraîche and caviar or a piece of smoked salmon at brunch. Or it would go well with plenty of the sauces from the Sawsawan chapter, like Sweet and Spicy Banana Ketchup (page 49) or Spicy Miso Tahini (page 54).

1. In a large bowl, combine the acorn squash, sweet potato, carrots, and green onions.

2. In a separate medium bowl, whisk together the chickpea flour, rice flour, salt, and seltzer water. Pour the batter into the vegetable mixture and mix until it's fully combined.

3. Pour the oil into a heavy 12 in [30.5 cm] cast-iron skillet. The oil should be about ½ in [13 mm] deep. Heat the oil until it reads 350°F [180°C] on a frying thermometer.

4. Using a ⅓ cup [80 ml] measuring cup, scoop the batter into the hot oil. Fry the cakes, 3 or 4 at a time to avoid overcrowding, for 3 minutes on each side until they turn a J. Lo golden brown and look crunchy. Transfer to a wire rack set on top of a baking sheet and season with salt while still hot. Repeat with the remaining batter.

5. Transfer the ukoy to a serving plate and sprinkle dill and cilantro on top. Serve with vinegar sauce for dipping. These are best enjoyed right away.

Lumpia

Lumpia is essentially a fried spring roll. It's a very common appetizer or snack food found at Filipino gatherings, and when I see lumpia, I know it's a special occasion. After all, frying something isn't that easy, so lumpia means someone put in some extra effort. I suggest buying premade spring roll wrappers—they're usually just flour, cornstarch, and water—because there's no good reason to make them from scratch, and most Asian markets have them readily available. And, anyway, the real star is what's inside—usually some sort of ground-up protein like chicken or pork, but sometimes just vegetables, and always with lots of yummy spices. The end result is a crispy, crackling outer layer filled with a mouthwatering, tasty nugget of savory deliciousness. It's like a little present. That's how I've always thought of them, since I was a child, the food version of a gift.

One of my favorite memories from childhood is sitting at the kitchen counter and watching my lola roll her lumpia, one by one. I love how making these for friends is carrying on my lola's legacy—so much of cooking is about nurturing and caring for people, and by cooking lumpia, I feel like I'm taking the love, comfort, and warmth she gave me and passing it on to my friends, family, and loved ones. It's taking her spirit and keeping it alive.

Kabocha Squash Lumpia

MAKES 25 LUMPIA, SERVES 6 TO 8

¼ cup [60 ml] extra-virgin olive oil

2 Tbsp unseasoned rice vinegar

2 Tbsp maple syrup

2 Tbsp Spicy Miso Tahini / RECIPE ON PAGE 54

2½ lb [1.2 kg] kabocha squash, seeded, peeled, and cut into rough 1 in [2.5 cm] cubes

2 carrots, roughly chopped into small pieces

1 shallot, roughly chopped

3 garlic cloves, minced

2 tsp kosher salt, plus more to taste

2 tsp togarashi or chili flakes

1 tsp white pepper

Juice of 1 lemon

¼ cup [5 g] finely chopped fresh chives

Twenty-five 8 in [20 cm] spring roll wrappers

Neutral oil, such as canola or grapeseed oil, for frying

There are a few different lumpia recipes in this book, but this one is my ode to fall flavors, adapted from a lumpia dish I made in 2020 for a Kamayan dinner (Kamayan is a traditional Filipino feast where the food is almost exclusively eaten with your hands). The star of this dish is certainly the kabocha squash, which is like if a pumpkin and a sweet potato had a baby. I just love it so much—it's sweet, nutty, hearty, and earthy.

Here, we roast the squash and get it all soft and squishy and then use that as the filling. Juxtaposed with the crunchy, crispy fried wrapper, it makes for such a fun contrast in textures and flavors. Lumpia are usually savory, so I like the touch of sweetness we add here with the squash and maple syrup. The whole thing is giving pumpkin spice latte, but Filipino-ish. Also, I do love the filling to be smooth, but sometimes if I want even more texture, I leave it just a touch lumpy so there are chunks of squash in the middle. Just another option, depending on how you feel.

1. Preheat the oven to 375°F [190°C] and place the rack in the middle of the oven.

2. In a large bowl, whisk together the olive oil, rice vinegar, maple syrup, and spicy miso tahini. Toss in the kabocha squash, carrots, shallot, garlic, salt, togarashi, and white pepper. With your clean bare hands, massage the marinade into the vegetable mixture until well coated. Dump the mixture onto a baking sheet and spread out the vegetables evenly.

3. Roast for 20 to 25 minutes until the squash is soft to the point where you can gently press a squash piece and it is easily smushed. Let the vegetables cool completely.

4. Transfer the vegetable mixture to a food processor. Pulse and then process for about 2 minutes until the mixture is slightly smooth and chunky. With a rubber spatula, scrape the mixture into a medium bowl. Taste and adjust the seasoning as needed. Add the lemon juice and fold in the chives. Scoop the vegetable mixture into a big zip-top plastic bag and push the mixture into one of the corners, leaving a space of about 2 in [5 cm] in the corner that you will snip off to pipe out the mixture onto the wrappers. Squeeze out as many air pockets as you can.

continued

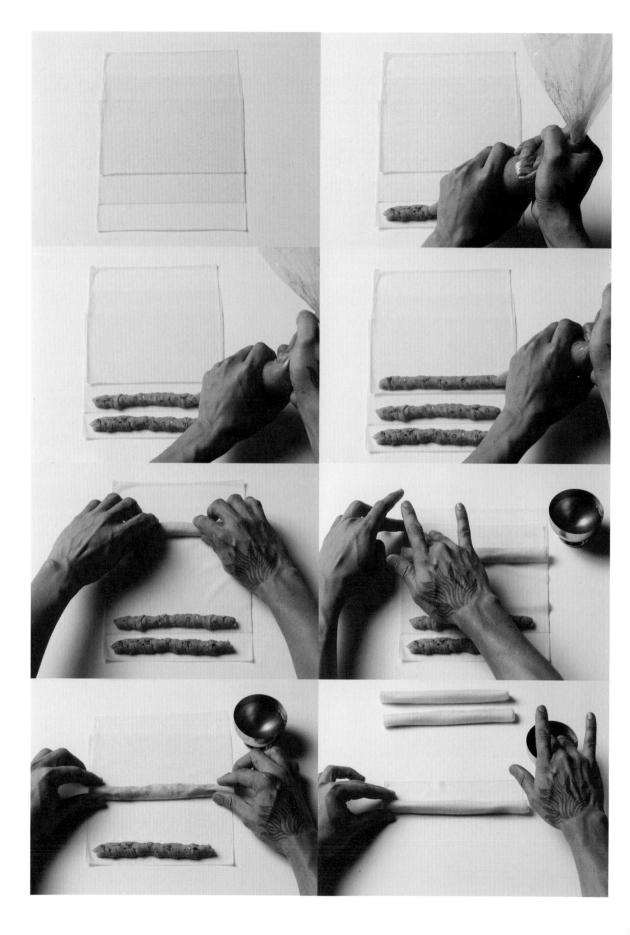

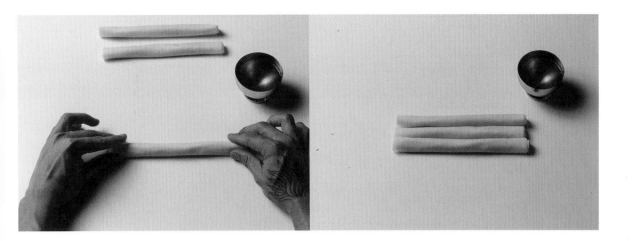

5. Place a small bowl of water near your work station. Line a rimmed baking sheet with paper towels.

6. Peel off 5 spring roll wrappers and lay them on a clean work surface. With kitchen shears, snip off the corner of the bag and pipe the mixture along the bottom of each sheet. Fill in one end to the other until each sheet is filled. You should be piping about 1½ Tbsp of the filling per wrapper. Roll each wrapper up, leaving 1 in [2.5 cm] at the end. With your clean fingertips, dab water on the overhang of the wrapper and roll to seal the lumpia. Transfer the lumpia seam side down onto the paper towel–lined baking sheet and cover with a damp cloth. Repeat with the remaining filling and wrappers.

7. At this point, you can freeze the lumpia if you are preparing them in advance. Lay the lumpia in a single layer on a parchment paper–lined baking sheet; make sure they are not touching so they don't stick to each other. Place the baking sheet uncovered in the freezer for 2 hours until they are firm. Transfer the frozen lumpia to freezer-safe bags. Label the bags with the date and store

in the freezer for up to 1 month. To cook frozen lumpia, add 2 to 3 minutes to the frying time.

8. Pour the neutral oil into a high-sided, heavy-bottom pan to a depth of 2 to 3 in [5 to 7.5 cm]. Heat over medium-high heat for about 7 minutes, or until it reads 350°F [180°C] on a frying thermometer.

9. Working in batches, fry 3 to 5 lumpia at a time, making sure not to crowd the pan. Fry each side for 3 to 5 minutes until crispy and a sensual golden-brown color. Transfer the lumpia to the paper towel–lined baking sheet and immediately season with salt. Transfer to a serving platter and enjoy them while they are hot and crispy! These are best eaten right away.

Quick Garlic Confit *with Coconut Labneh*

SERVES 4

2 cups [455 g] Coconut Labneh / RECIPE ON PAGE 44

Zest and juice of 1 lemon

1 garlic clove, grated

Quick Garlic Confit / RECIPE ON PAGE 64

1 Tbsp crushed pink peppercorns

1 Tbsp Easy Crispy Garlic / RECIPE ON PAGE 57, or store-bought

¼ cup [5 g] roughly chopped dill

Fresh vegetables, crackers, and crusty bread, for serving

If there's one thing Filipinos love, it's their garlic. This recipe is my love letter to this humble ingredient, and it's a real treat for my garlic enthusiasts out there. Just . . . keep a mint handy.

This sumptuous, elegant dip is great served with crackers, crispy fall crudités like celery or carrots, or a fresh loaf of crusty bread that's been torn up. I'm telling you, the contrast of the pillowy coconut labneh with the full-flavored, luscious garlic . . . this dip will be gone in an instant.

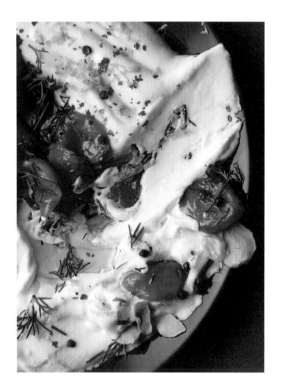

In a medium bowl, mix together the coconut labneh, lemon zest, lemon juice, and grated garlic. Spread the coconut labneh into a shallow bowl and make a well in the middle with the back of a spoon. Using a clean spoon, place 5 to 7 confit garlic cloves (or more to your heart's desire) on top with about 1 Tbsp of the garlic oil. Sprinkle with crushed pink peppercorns and crispy garlic and garnish with dill. Serve with fresh crudités, crackers, or crusty bread! Store in an airtight container in the refrigerator for up to 3 days.

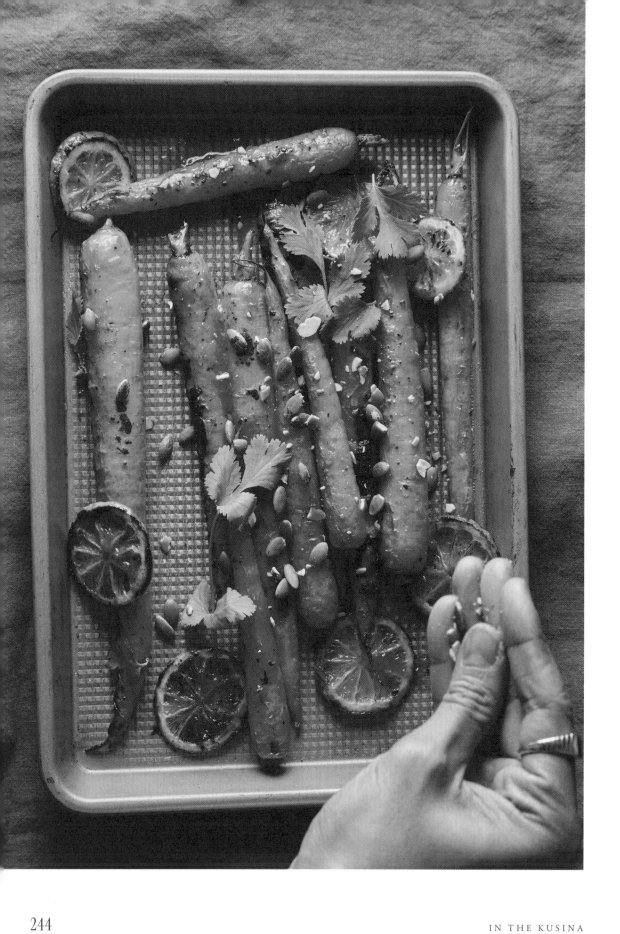

Sweet and Spicy Banana-Ketchup Roasted Carrots

SERVES 4

2 lb [910 g] carrots

2 garlic cloves, grated

One 1 in [2.5 cm] piece fresh ginger, peeled and grated

1 lime, thinly sliced

2 Tbsp extra-virgin olive oil

Kosher salt

Freshly ground black pepper

½ cup [120 g] Sweet and Spicy Banana Ketchup / RECIPE ON PAGE 49

¼ cup [35 g] pumpkin seeds, toasted

Sweet and Spicy Banana Ketchup is perfect for roasting autumnal vegetables. Not only does its flavor profile pair beautifully—the sweet-umami-spicy trio brings out a carrot's natural honeyed essence—but it gives it this shiny, candied look. And then the lime juice adds a zippity bite, and some toasted pumpkin seeds sprinkled on top give it *juuuuust* the right amount of crunch. A side dish that will have the crowd going wild.

1. Preheat the oven to 425°F [220°C].

2. In a roasting pan, toss the carrots with the garlic, ginger, lime, and olive oil. Season with salt and pepper, then pour the banana ketchup over the carrots. With your clean hands, toss the carrots with the sauce until well coated.

3. Roast the carrots for 35 to 40 minutes until the carrots are tender and the limes are caramelized.

4. Sprinkle the carrots with the toasted pumpkin seeds and serve right away.

Caraflex Cabbage
with Almond Goldenberry Gremolata

SERVES 2

1 head Caraflex cabbage, quartered

Kosher salt

Freshly ground black pepper

3 Tbsp avocado oil

Almond Goldenberry Gremolata / RECIPE ON PAGE 60

Flaky sea salt

1. On a baking sheet, season the cabbage with kosher salt and pepper.

2. Heat a sauté pan or cast-iron skillet over high heat and add the avocado oil. Gently place the cabbage into the skillet and sear until charred and crisp on both sides, about 3 minutes per side. Transfer the cabbage to a plate.

3. Drizzle the almond goldenberry gremolata over the cabbage and provide her with a happy ending of flaky salt sprinkled right on top. Serve right away!

I am a cabbage lover, a cabbage advocate, a cabbage truther! I think cabbage has gotten a bad rap over the years, but one of my life's missions is to show people that she's an amazing girl and deserves to be worshipped. I love to char and sear her; it gives her a crunchy, smoky exterior flavor but preserves that mild, sweet cabbage flavor inside. In other words, it helps reveal her versatile, multifaceted nature. I love a Caraflex cabbage because of its darling little conical shape—it reminds me of that movie *Coneheads* that I used to watch a lot when I was a kid.

Smother the cabbage with the gremolata, making sure to get her in all the nooks and crannies. Cabbage tends to have a subtler taste; the gremolata brings the flavor and texture to this party. For such a simple dish, this really packs a lot of excitement. If there are any cabbage doubters out there, try this. I think you'll be a convert.

Roasted Brussels Sprouts
with Miso Tahini and Pomegranate Seeds

SERVES 4

1 lb [455 g] Brussels sprouts, trimmed and halved

2 Tbsp extra-virgin olive oil

Kosher salt

1 lime

2 Tbsp Spicy Miso Tahini / RECIPE ON PAGE 54

1 Tbsp toasted black sesame seeds

2 Tbsp pomegranate seeds

1. Preheat the oven to 450°F [230°C].

2. On a baking sheet, toss the Brussels sprouts with the olive oil and season with salt to taste. Spread out the Brussels sprouts with the cut sides down evenly on the baking sheet. Roast for 10 to 15 minutes until the cut sides are crunchy and she's golden brown like Beyoncé!

3. Transfer the Brussels sprouts to a serving platter. Zest and juice the lime all over the top, then drizzle with the spicy miso tahini. Sprinkle the sprouts with the sesame seeds and finish her off with a showering of pomegranate seeds. Store leftovers in an airtight container in the refrigerator for up to 3 days.

I love Brussels sprouts because they're like mini cabbages, and when you roast them, they get all soft and mushy inside and then have these crunchy exterior leaves, which is so fun. Here, I pair them with a velvety miso-tahini sauce that adds a nice earthy, grounded umami flavor, and the whipped texture is a fun complement to those crispy leaves. My favorite part, though, is the dazzling rubies of pomegranate seeds. Seriously, it's like adding jewelry to your food, it's so beautiful—and then when you're eating it, it's a little crunch followed by a burst of tart juice in your mouth. It's kind of naughty but oh-so-fun to eat, and the perfect sharp little moment to lighten the dish. I think eating food should be a joyful act, and this dish is exactly that.

Fall

Sweet and Sour Roasted Squash
with Pickled Golden Raisins and Coconut Labneh

SERVES 4

SQUASH

2 delicata squash, halved lengthwise, seeded, and sliced into 1 in [2.5 cm] half-moons

3 garlic cloves, minced

3 Tbsp extra-virgin olive oil

Kosher salt

Freshly ground black pepper

SAUCE

½ cup [120 g] sweet chili sauce

½ cup [120 ml] apple cider vinegar

2 Tbsp tamari

ASSEMBLY

Coconut Labneh / RECIPE ON PAGE 44

1 to 2 Tbsp Pickled Golden Raisins / RECIPE ON PAGE 62

½ cup [10 g] cilantro leaves

When I was growing up, we didn't really roast that often; my mom and dad mostly cooked on the stovetop. But now that I live in the Northeast, I've discovered the wonders of roasting. It's such an incredible way to impart flavor and texture to things, mostly vegetables and proteins, and I've come to think of it as a warm, cocooning, cozy sweater for your meal.

So, the roasted squash is the real centerpiece here, but this dish is the epitome of how I like to cook in that there's a lot of very different elements competing but in a very harmonious way. Sorry, but I want lots of texture and flavor! And this dish delivers—from the very sweet-sour-salty marinade on the squash to the refreshing, glossy-smooth labneh it sits on to the tart and juicy golden raisins sprinkled on top. She's a very over-the-top dish, which you need sometimes, especially as the days get shorter. I think of bringing this as a side to a big group meal and then being like, "Oops, she's actually stealing the spotlight, my bad!" LOL. Anyway, for a humble roast vegetable, this baby really is a showstopper.

1. Preheat oven to 375°F [190°C].

2. TO MAKE THE SQUASH: On a baking sheet, add the delicata squash and garlic. Drizzle with the olive oil and season with salt and pepper to taste. Using your clean hands, massage and mix the squash to get it nicely coated and seasoned. Lay out the squash flat and evenly spaced on the baking sheet. Roast for about 15 minutes, then flip and roast the other side for another 12 minutes, or until tender and caramelized. Let the squash cool for about 10 minutes before serving.

3. TO MAKE THE SAUCE: While the squash is roasting, in a small saucepan, whisk together the sweet chili sauce, apple cider vinegar,

and tamari. Set over medium heat and bring to a simmer, stirring occasionally, until she becomes thick and syrupy, 8 to 10 minutes. Set aside.

4. TO ASSEMBLE: On a round serving platter, take a giant heaping spoonful of coconut labneh and blob her right in the middle of the platter. Schmear the coconut labneh in a gyrating circular motion to create a pool for the squash to rest on. Lay the squash haphazardly right on top of the coconut labneh. Take the sauce and drizzle it over the squash to give her a nice, shiny coating. Sprinkle the raisins over the squash. Garnish with the cilantro and serve! This dish is best eaten right away.

Fall

Fall Chop Suey *with Ginger Sauce*

SERVES 4 TO 6

3 Tbsp avocado oil

1 shallot, minced

1 Tbsp peeled and minced fresh ginger

3 garlic cloves, minced

12 oz [340 g] shiitake mushrooms, stemmed and caps sliced

1 cup [120 g] sliced carrot

1 cup [120 g] sliced celery

3 Tbsp Ginger Sauce / RECIPE ON PAGE 55

Kosher salt

Freshly ground black pepper

1 tsp sesame oil

1 tsp toasted sesame seeds

½ cup [10 g] cilantro leaves

Stovetop Jasmine Rice / RECIPE ON PAGE 75 or plain noodles, for serving

Chop suey is a vegetable stir-fry with some protein added in. I think it pairs well with heartier, earthy fall vegetables like carrots and celery. And then, instead of meat, I use chewy, umami-packed shiitake mushrooms. What I love about this dish is it's just so easy and filling. It's a good weeknight no-fuss meal.

What really makes this dish sing, though, is the ginger sauce. It's a take on the Filipino all-purpose sauce, which is this brown gravy that usually comes in a bottle and has a bit of heat. So here, I use the ginger to bring in that comforting, warming quality. You could serve this with rice or egg noodles too. It's just such an easy go-to, I think you'll find yourself making it a few times a week.

1. In a large sauté pan over medium-high heat, warm the avocado oil. Sauté the shallot and ginger for about 2 minutes; you'll immediately start to smell them caramelizing. Add the garlic and shiitake mushrooms. Stir together and cook for about 5 minutes until the juices from the mushrooms start to gush into the pan. At this point, sprinkle in the carrot and celery. Stir all the vegetables together and cook for 3 to 5 more minutes.

2. Pour in the ginger sauce and ¼ cup [60 ml] of water and stir. Season with salt and pepper. Bring to a simmer, then remove from the heat. Drizzle in the sesame oil and sprinkle with the sesame seeds. Shower the stir-fry with the cilantro and serve with rice. Voilà! Store leftovers in an airtight container in the refrigerator for up to 3 days.

Bicol Express Cauliflower
with Golden Raisin Gremolata

SERVES 4

Kosher salt

1 head cauliflower (2 to 2½ lb [910 g to 1.2 kg])

2 Tbsp avocado oil

1 small shallot, chopped

2 garlic cloves, minced

1 Tbsp peeled and minced fresh ginger

2 Thai chiles, thinly sliced

1½ Tbsp Miso Mushroom Bagoong / RECIPE ON PAGE 54

One 14 oz [420 ml] can unsweetened coconut milk

Golden Raisin Gremolata / RECIPE ON PAGE 61, for garnish

Stovetop Jasmine Rice / RECIPE ON PAGE 75, for serving

1. In a large pot big enough to fit the whole head of cauliflower, bring 6 qt [5.7 L] of water to a boil. Season the boiling water generously with salt. The boiling water should taste like salty ocean water. Place the cauliflower stem side up in the boiling water. Cook for 6 to 8 minutes until tender.

2. Place a colander in the sink and transfer the cauliflower to the colander with the head facing down so the water can drain off. Let it drain for about 10 minutes.

3. Preheat the oven to 400°F [200°C].

4. Meanwhile, in a large oven-safe sauté pan over medium heat, warm the avocado oil. Sauté the shallot for about 3 minutes. Throw in the garlic, ginger, and chiles. Stir and cook for 3 to 5 minutes until fragrant. Whisk in the miso mushroom bagoong and pour in the coconut milk. Stir everything together and bring to a simmer. Let cook at a gentle simmer for 5 to 7 minutes until the flavors have melded together.

5. Transfer the cauliflower to a clean cutting board and cut the cauliflower in half. Season with kosher salt and transfer the two halves cut side down to the awaiting pool of simmering coconut milk. Transfer the pan to the oven and roast for 20 to 25 minutes until the cauliflower reaches caramelization status.

6. Transfer the cauliflower to a serving platter. Spoon all the coconut sauce over the cauliflower and garnish with the gremolata. Serve with a bowl of rice. Store leftovers in an airtight container in the refrigerator for up to 3 days.

Bicol is a dish named after a region of the Philippines known for its spicy foods. It's traditionally a protein stewed in coconut milk and a bunch of aromatics like garlic, ginger, and chile. I use cauliflower because there's a ton of it around in the fall and it has a heft that feels really nourishing for the season.

In the spring and summer chapters, you'll notice we do a lot of really simple, fresh, elegant dishes that honor the ingredients, but this is a good example of a fall dish that requires a bit more time and TLC. But I think that's right for the season, where it's colder and you may be at home anyway, staying cozy. So if this is a bit more of an involved preparation, embrace that and lean into it. That's how you get these really rich, layered, overlapping flavors—and you definitely get that with this. It's a super hearty, hefty, creamy stew, and then we add the golden raisin gremolata to add a bit of vibrancy and chew as a balance.

Pancit Adobo

SERVES 4 TO 6

½ cup [120 ml] white vinegar

½ cup [120 ml] soy sauce

¼ cup [60 ml] dark maple syrup

1 Tbsp freshly ground black pepper

3 Tbsp neutral oil, such as canola or grapeseed oil

5 garlic cloves, finely minced

4 cups [960 ml] low-sodium vegetable stock

1 lb [455 g] bihon (see Note)

3 green onions, sliced on a bias

2 Tbsp Easy Crispy Garlic / RECIPE ON PAGE 57, or store-bought

½ cup [10 g] cilantro leaves and stems, for garnish

2 limes, quartered, for serving

1. In a medium bowl, whisk together the vinegar, soy sauce, maple syrup, and black pepper to make an adobo sauce. Set aside.

2. In a large pot over medium heat, warm the oil, then add the garlic. Sauté until fragrant, about 3 minutes. Add the vegetable stock and adobo sauce and stir with a wooden spoon. Bring her to a boil. At this point, you'll start to smell the pungent peppery adobo sauce.

3. Submerge the bihon in the sauce and cook for 3 to 5 minutes. When the noodles reach the point where you can take the tongs and wiggle them around the pan, that's when you know the adobo sauce is being soaked up. Stir constantly until the liquid has evaporated.

4. Remove the pot from the heat, sprinkle in the green onions, and mix together until you see specks of green onions poking out from the pancit.

5. Transfer the pancit to a gorgeous platter. Shower the dish with the crispy garlic and garnish with the cilantro. To serve, squeeze fresh lime juice over the top, grab a fork, and dig in! Store leftovers in an airtight container in the refrigerator for up to 3 days.

Step aside, traditional adobo, there's a new noodle sheriff in town! Introducing Pancit Adobo, the dish that decided life was too short for plain old rice. Imagine the savory seduction of classic adobo cozying up to the slurp-worthy allure of tender bihon (a.k.a. thin rice noodles). It's a flavor fiesta for your taste buds, complete with a confetti of green onions and herby cilantro. Warning: May induce uncontrollable happiness and the occasional giggle fit. Proceed with fork or chopsticks at the ready!

NOTE: Bihon are a type of thin rice noodle. If you can't find bihon at your local market or Asian grocer, substitute vermicelli noodles.

Spiced Pumpkin Cake *with Coconut Glaze*

MAKES ONE 8½ BY 4½ IN [21.5 BY 11 CM] LOAF

PUMPKIN LOAF

¾ cup [105 g] all-purpose flour

¾ cup [105 g] whole wheat flour

1 tsp kosher salt

1 tsp baking soda

1 tsp ginger powder

1 cup [225 g] pumpkin purée

⅓ cup [80 ml] maple syrup

3 Tbsp fresh peeled and grated ginger

2 tsp Chinese five-spice powder

1 tsp vanilla extract

8 oz [230 g] unsalted butter, at room temperature

½ cup [120 g] coconut palm sugar

2 eggs, at room temperature

½ cup [120 g] sour cream, at room temperature

COCONUT GLAZE

1⅓ cups [160 g] confectioners' sugar

½ tsp kosher salt, preferably Diamond Crystal

¼ cup [60 ml] unsweetened coconut milk, plus more as needed

1 tsp fresh lemon juice

½ cup [70 g] crystallized ginger, chopped, for decoration

This is my ode to all those girls who love an infinity scarf and Ugg boots—we all have a pumpkin spice girlie in us, myself included, and she definitely wants this cake. The madness for pumpkin spice during this season is kinda eye roll-y, but it's also so funny at this point. So this is me embracing my love for pumpkin spice—because, guess what? I *am* that girl!

But of course, I have to Woldy-ize it, so I add Chinese five-spice powder and fresh and powdered ginger to impart a little intrigue and excitement. It provides this tingly, spicy heat—a tantalizing, prickly sensation that you won't find in any other cakes, I promise. I finish it off with a coconut glaze. It's unique but, at the end of the day, it's also just a delicious cake that delivers on warming, spiced goodness. Enjoy a slice with some hot tea for ultimate comfort.

continued

1. TO MAKE THE PUMPKIN LOAF: Preheat the oven to 350°F [180°C] and place the rack in the middle of the oven. Spray an 8½ by 4½ in [21.5 by 11 cm] loaf pan with nonstick spray and line it with parchment paper, leaving an inch or two overhang on either side for easy removal.

2. In a medium bowl, sift together both flours, the salt, baking soda, and ginger powder.

3. In a separate medium bowl, add the pumpkin purée, maple syrup, grated ginger, Chinese five-spice powder, and vanilla. Whisk together until she is lusciously smooth.

4. In the bowl of a stand mixer fitted with the whisk attachment, or using a large bowl and electric hand mixer, cream together the butter and coconut palm sugar on high speed until fluffy, 3 to 5 minutes.

5. Decrease the speed to medium and add the eggs one at a time, mixing until fully incorporated before adding the next one. Add the sour cream and mix to combine. Slowly pour in the pumpkin mixture. Decrease the speed to low and slowly add the flour mixture. Mix until fully combined and it becomes a smooth bottom, I mean batter.

6. Transfer the batter to the prepared loaf pan. Place the loaf pan on a baking sheet and bake the cake for 1 hour, or until a toothpick inserted into the center comes out clean.

7. Let the cake cool in the pan for 10 minutes. Pop the cake out of the loaf pan, using the parchment paper to help lift it out, and transfer it to a wire cooling rack with a baking sheet underneath. Let cool completely.

8. TO MAKE THE COCONUT GLAZE: In a medium bowl, whisk together the confectioners' sugar, salt, coconut milk, and lemon juice until smooth. If the consistency of the glaze is too thick, thin it out with a splash of coconut milk.

9. Pour the glaze all over the top of the cooled cake and immediately decorate with the chopped crystallized ginger. Let the cake sit for about 10 minutes before gobbling her up! Wrap leftovers tightly in plastic wrap or store in an airtight container at room temperature for up to 3 days.

Fall

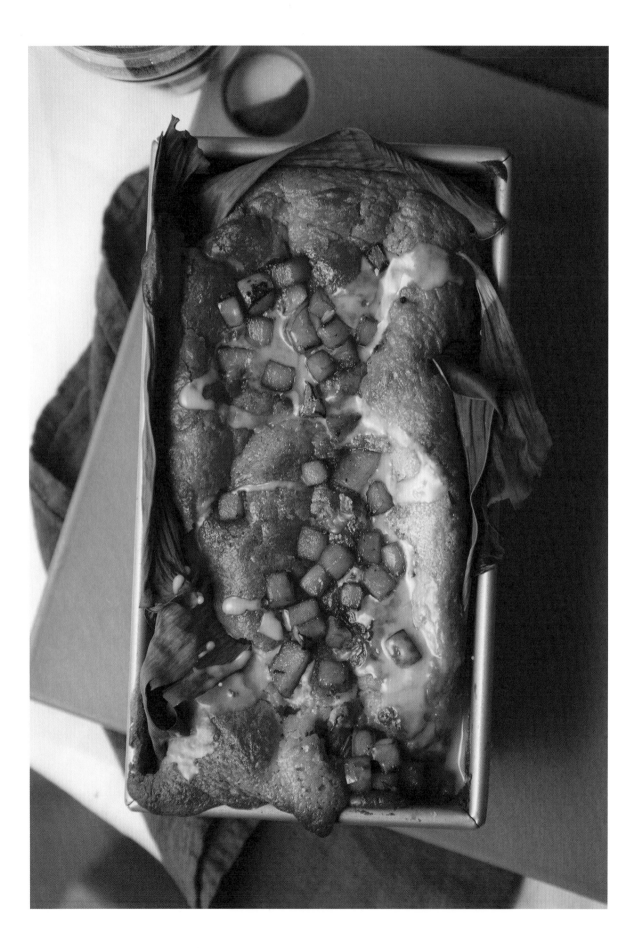

Bibingka Apple Bread *with Maple Glaze*

MAKES ONE 8½ BY 4½ IN [21.5 BY 11 CM] LOAF

APPLE BREAD

One 14 by 12 in [35.5 by 30.5 cm] banana leaf

1¼ cups [170 g] rice flour

1¼ cups [165 g] glutinous rice flour

1 cup [200 g] granulated sugar

1 Tbsp baking powder

1 tsp kosher salt

1 tsp ground cinnamon

¼ tsp ground nutmeg

3 eggs, at room temperature

One 14 oz [420 ml] can unsweetened coconut milk

1 cup [240 g] applesauce

½ cup [110 g] unrefined coconut oil, melted

1 tsp vanilla extract

2 cups [220 g] diced apple

MAPLE GLAZE

1 cup [125 g] confectioners' sugar

3 Tbsp maple syrup

1 Tbsp applesauce

½ tsp kosher salt

Add this to the list of recipes that really embody my Filipino American identity. This takes the idea of apple pie—a classic American dish if ever there was one—and adds in some Filipino flair. Then, on top of all that, I add in my autumn girl fantasies, and *voilà*!

We love this baby because she's got a dramatic presentation and lots of festive fall flavors. This recipe is like if leaf peeping were edible; I mean, apple, maple, and cinnamon are quintessential fall flavors. The coconut milk adds a tropical vibe that makes it special, and then the real game-changer is the banana leaf wrapping. When you take the loaf out of the oven, it's like this little island-y gift that you open up. All this steam rises from it, and this really heady, lovely aroma instantly fills the air. It's like fall, but in the tropics!

continued

1. **TO MAKE THE APPLE BREAD:** If the banana leaf is frozen, bring it to room temperature. Preheat the oven to 350°F [180°C] and position the rack in the middle of the oven. Spray a standard 8½ by 4½ in [21.5 by 11 cm] loaf pan with nonstick coconut oil cooking spray.

2. Using scissors, cut a 12 by 4 in [30.5 by 10 cm] strip from the banana leaf piece, cutting parallel to the leaf's center vein. Cut the remaining portion of the banana leaf into three 12 by 3 in [30.5 by 7.5 cm] strips, again cutting parallel to the leaf's vein. Wipe down each side of the leaves with a damp paper towel.

3. Place the 3 in [7.5 cm] wide banana leaf strips crosswise over the bottom and sides of the loaf pan, overlapping as needed to completely line the bottom of the pan. Make sure the leaf ends extend over the sides by 1 to 2 in [2.5 to 5 cm]. Place the remaining long banana leaf strip lengthwise along the bottom of the loaf pan and partway up the shorter sides. Set the pan aside.

4. In a large bowl, whisk together the rice flour, glutinous rice flour, granulated sugar, baking powder, salt, cinnamon, and nutmeg.

5. In a medium bowl, whisk together the eggs, coconut milk, applesauce, melted coconut oil, and vanilla. Whisk the wet ingredients into the dry ingredients until the mixture is fully incorporated and the batter is smooth.

6. Pour the batter into the prepared loaf pan and evenly sprinkle 1 cup [110 g] of the diced apple on top of the batter. Bake for 1 hour. Pull the loaf from the oven and sprinkle the remaining 1 cup [110 g] of diced apple on top of the loaf. Bake for an additional 10 to 15 minutes, until the apples are caramelized and the edges are glowy and golden and a wooden skewer inserted into the center comes out clean.

7. Let the cake cool in the pan for 10 minutes. To remove the bread from the loaf pan, gently lift the banana leaves from the sides and transfer the loaf to a wire cooling rack with a baking sheet underneath. Let the cake cool completely.

8. **TO MAKE THE MAPLE GLAZE:** In a small bowl, whisk together the confectioners' sugar, maple syrup, applesauce, and salt until smooth. Pour the glaze over the cooled apple bibingka. Slice and serve! Wrap leftovers tightly in plastic wrap or store in an airtight container at room temperature for up to 3 days.

Chocolate Bibingka

MAKES ONE 9 IN [23 CM] ROUND CAKE

1¼ cups [170 g] rice flour

1¼ cups [165 g] glutinous rice flour

1 cup [200 g] sugar

¾ cup [75 g] cocoa powder

1 Tbsp baking powder

1 tsp kosher salt

3 eggs, at room temperature

One 14 oz [420 ml] can unsweetened coconut milk

1 cup [240 ml] sweetened condensed milk

1 tsp vanilla extract

6 oz [170 g] 70% dark chocolate, roughly chopped

½ cup [110 g] unsalted butter

Chocolate Coconut Mousse / RECIPE ON PAGE 116, for garnish (optional)

Confectioners' sugar, for garnish (optional)

1. Preheat the oven to 350°F [180°C] and position the rack in the middle of the oven. Spray a 9 by 2 in [23 by 5 cm] round cake pan with nonstick olive oil cooking spray.

2. In a large bowl, whisk together the rice flour, glutinous rice flour, sugar, cocoa powder, baking powder, and salt.

3. In a medium bowl, whisk together the eggs, coconut milk, sweetened condensed milk, and vanilla. Set aside.

4. In a small saucepan over medium-low heat, melt the chocolate and butter together. Gently stir until the mixture is completely smooth.

5. Pour the chocolate mixture into the wet ingredients and whisk until incorporated and smooth. Pour the wet ingredients into the dry ingredients and whisk until the batter is smooth.

6. Pour the batter into the prepared cake pan and bake for 1 hour, or until a wooden skewer inserted into the center comes out clean.

7. Let the cake cool in the pan for 10 minutes. Remove the cake from the pan and transfer to a wire cooling rack with a baking sheet underneath. Let cool completely, then transfer the cake to a cake stand. Slice and serve with a generous scoop of chocolate mousse and a dusting of confectioners' sugar, if desired. Wrap leftovers tightly in plastic wrap or store in an airtight container at room temperature for up to 3 days.

To be totally honest, I was just bored one day and got to thinking about how I could evolve bibingka or spin it in a new direction (this is what chefs do when they have too much time on their hands!). And, duh, *chocolate*. Chocolate makes everything better. But the lightbulb moment was when I asked myself: *What if I made bibingka like a brownie?!* Like a classic Betty Crocker, from-the-box mix sort of thing. So here I've added not one but two different chocolate elements: cocoa powder and rich, slightly bitter melted dark chocolate. Try not to swoon! By blending a classic chocolate brownie with traditional bibingka, it's sort of like this encapsulation of me: part American, part Filipino, totally fabulous.

Fall

Acknowledgments

With all my heart, I want to begin by thanking my family: my mom Emma (I LOVE YOU), my dad Wilfredo (I hope you're looking down on us with pride), my brother Randy, and my twin brother Wally and his wife Jessel. A special thanks to my beloved lola. I dedicate this cookbook to Lola Dominga, whose kusina and home garden sparked my love for food and cooking. Your stories, beauty, and home-cooked Filipino dishes inspired me to become the chef I am today. To my titas, Becky and Oyie, for being strong women and instilling resilience in me, and to the entire Aguirre and Reyes family for their support and encouragement throughout my life.

This book wouldn't have been possible without the incredible team that brought it all together. A special thanks to Adriana Stimola, my literary agent, who made a beeline toward me in a crowded room at *Cherry Bombe*'s Jubilee in 2022 and introduced herself by saying, "I know who you are," before handing me her card. Your belief in me and in this book means the world to me, and I am forever grateful. To Max Berlinger, who was instrumental in ghostwriting the proposal and the book. Together, we navigated this journey, and I trusted you to help bring my words to life and keep me on track throughout the process! Cristina Garces, who believed in this book from the very beginning—I am eternally grateful for bringing me into the Chronicle family. To my editors, Claire Gilhuly and Cara Bedick, thank you for keeping me accountable, even as I repeatedly requested deadline extensions. Lizzie Vaughan, designing this book with you has been an incredibly rewarding experience. You gave me so much creative freedom, and I'm deeply thankful for the opportunity. I believe we've created something truly beautiful together. Arsh Raziuddin, thank you for the artful illustration of my family—you added a touch of romance to the book that means so much to me. To the incredible creative team who brought the visual story to life—Fujio Emura, LJ Almendras, Tony Ortiz, Sasha Veryovka, Seth Kenji, Lauren Holmquist, Kate Atkinson, and Tara Thomas—those twelve-hour days and shooting sixteen to eighteen images a day truly pushed us all to our creative limits. Despite the challenges we faced, we grew together as individuals, and I'm grateful for the journey we shared.

I want to take a moment to express my deep appreciation and love to Tara Thomas. Your unwavering support, countless hours of brainstorming, and collaboration made this journey more fun and intentional. Thank you, darling!

I'm deep in gratitude to the friends and colleagues who dedicated their time to recipe testing and offered valuable feedback to improve the recipes. Your insights have been instrumental in creating this cookbook. Special thanks to LJ Almendras, Danielle Van Noy and Gordon Waltho, Jordan Smith, Kendal Duff, Ryan Del Franco, Sam Sabol, Sophia Aerts, and Filip Ševo.

To my partners who generously contributed to this cookbook and helped bring my vision to life: Thank you to Bob's Red Mill, Brightland, Burlap & Barrel, Cocojune, Hawkins New York, Heermance Farm (Marika and Neil Bender), Jacobsen Salt Co. (The James Collective), Koda Farms, Laurel & Ash Farm, M-W NYC (Melody Anderson), Seed + Mill, Simple Mills, SOUTHEAST Asia Food Group, West~Bourne (Camilla Marcus), Aplós, S. Pellegrino S.p.A. (Anna Mandelbaum), Fazeek, Hudson Wilder, Material Kitchen (Eunice Byun), Staub, ZWILLING, Audi, and Hooker Green (Jordan and Paul Ferney).

A special shout out to the folks whose encouragement, guidance, and continued support have helped me navigate to this point in my career. This cookbook is a testament to always showing up and doing the work. All of you have a special place in my heart. Andrea Gentyl, Martin Hyers, Andrea Ng, Andrew Corrigan, Anna Polonsky and Fernando Aciar, Caroline Aquino, Edy Massish, Emily Johnson, Nick Cameron and Olive, Erika Mercado, Geoffrey Aquino, Jordan Potter, Kerry Diamond, Kristen Barnett, Laura Ferrera, Maria Arrington, Mariana Velasquez and Diego Senor, Maryah Ananda, Nicole Ponseca, Noreen Wasti, One Love Community Fridge, Pri Aguilar, Sara Byworth and Jillian Farina, Sara Keene, Susan Spungen, and Zaynab Issa.

I am deeply grateful to the early supporters of Woldy Kusina, the catering business I launched in 2016. It was an exciting yet daunting time as I made the leap from fashion to food. You all gave me the motivation to wake up early, step into the kitchen, and do what I love most—cooking and delivering meals to your homes, offices, backstage at fashion shows, or glitzy showrooms to impress editors.

My heartfelt thanks go to Alexandra Gordon, Alicia Yates, Alison Egan, Allison Vartolo, Bernadette Pascua, Betsy Stanglmayr, Catherine Smith Licari, Cristian Candmill, Daniel Clurman, Barbara Clurman, Deborah Check, Fatima Bautista, Gayle Dizon and Dizon Inc., Jessie Randall, Kristina Rutkowski, Marysia and Nathaniel Reeves, MATCHESFASHION, Natasha Stanglmayr and Martine Mulder, Payton Kampschroer, Peter Stanglmayr and Marion Kassaei, Pioneer Works, Rebecca Minkoff, Rebekah Rutkowski, Samantha Moray, Suwatana Kamutchat Rycroft, Ulla Johnson and Zach Miner, and Zimmermann.

Chronicle Books, thank you for giving me the opportunity to share my story and my food with the world. I'm incredibly grateful!

To the supportive community that has followed my culinary journey, I hope this book nourishes and enlightens you, and offers a chance to connect with others through the art of cooking.

Maraming salamat—thank you!

Index

276

Index

Index

Woldy Reyes is a chef, tastemaker, and the founder of the boutique catering company Woldy Kusina, based in Brooklyn. Recognized as one of New York City's top chefs, Woldy has been featured in *Vogue*, *Bon Appétit*, the *New Yorker*, *Goop*, and *Food & Wine*, and has worked with brands including J.Crew, West Elm, Saie, and Well+Good. As a first-generation Filipino American, Woldy infuses contemporary dishes with vibrant flavors and colors inspired by his roots. He splits his time between Brooklyn and upstate New York.

Chronicle Books publishes distinctive books and gifts. From award-winning children's titles, bestselling cookbooks, and eclectic pop culture to acclaimed works of art and design, stationery, and journals, we craft publishing that's instantly recognizable for its spirit and creativity. Enjoy our publishing and become part of our community at www.chroniclebooks.com.

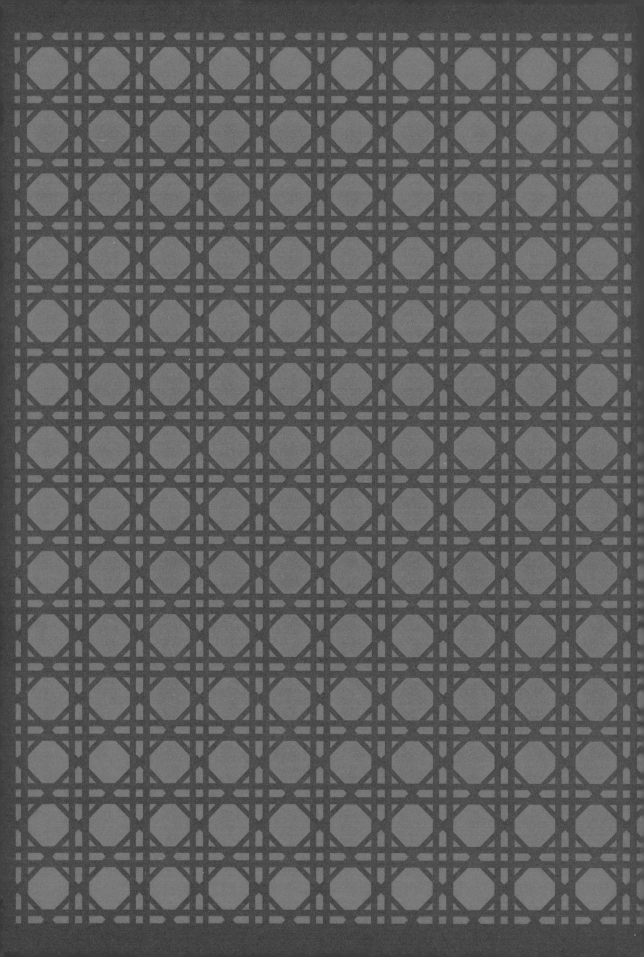